Beowulf Sheehan

Rowan Ricardo Phillips is the author of three books of poems (*Living Weapon*, *Heaven*, and *The Ground*) and the essay collection *When Blackness Rhymes with Blackness*. His awards include the Whiting Writers' Award, the PEN/Joyce Osterweil Award, the Anisfield-Wolf Book Award, the PEN/ESPN Award for Literary Sports Writing, the Nicolás Guillén Outstanding Book Award, and a Guggenheim Fellowship. He lives in New York City and Barcelona.

Praise for *The Circuit*

"For those who follow tennis, *The Circuit* is the book to read. With sharp insight into the key players' mannerisms, dazzling physical description, and lyrical, gorgeous prose, it's a pure treat. Rowan Ricardo Phillips's passion for the sport, its subtle geometries and self-defeating head games, is unequaled: game, set, match."

—Phillip Lopate, author of *To Show and To Tell*

"The revered poet and essayist Rowan Ricardo Phillips makes a thrilling tarot of the world's iconic tennis tournaments and reads past and future champions of that Darwinian tour as its players circumnavigate the globe. But who won't find Phillips mining their own fears and aspirations in the lives he captures off court or between points? By injury or age, we are all headed for some metaphorical sideline, and the genius of this book is that the fortunes Phillips evokes sagely, cannily, have always been ours."

—Gregory Pardlo, Pulitzer Prize–winning author of *Digest*

"Phillips keeps the pages turning with an easy yet exacting style and keen observations. Tennis nerds in particular will enjoy his parsing of Federer's retooled backhand . . . Phillips's wit suffuses this text . . . *The Circuit* is a welcome palate cleanser, a license to enjoy an underrated sport at its best. It's a love letter that looks to inspire a new generation of fans to watch through the darkness, and to motivate the older zealots among us to keep spreading the gospel to all corners."

—Andrew Lawrence, *The Atlantic*

"As an aficionado and player, Phillips is especially attuned to tennis's weirdness among other sports . . . Phillips's lyrical impulses ignite his compressed, efficient, accurate, lively and always liquid prose . . . Phillips wields his prose like an elegant, one-handed backhand, fending off florid metaphors and deflecting the canards about sports, to present the tour's basic process: the sport is a distraction."

—Walton Muyumba, *Los Angeles Times*

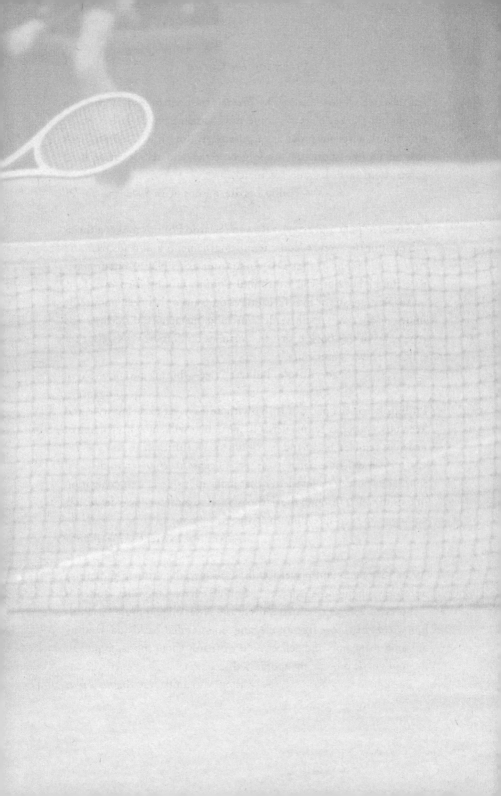

THE CIRCUIT

A Tennis Odyssey

ROWAN RICARDO PHILLIPS

PICADOR | FARRAR, STRAUS AND GIROUX | NEW YORK

Picador
120 Broadway, New York 10271

Grateful acknowledgment is made for permission to reprint an excerpt
from "Why I Am Not a Painter" from *The Collected Poems of Frank O'Hara*
by Frank O'Hara, copyright © 1971 by Maureen Granville-Smith,
Administratrix of the Estate of Frank O'Hara, copyright renewed 1999 by
Maureen O'Hara Granville-Smith and Donald Allen. Used by permission
of Alfred A. Knopf, an imprint of the Knopf Doubleday Publishing Group,
a division of Penguin Random House LLC. All rights reserved.

The Library of Congress has cataloged the Farrar, Straus and Giroux
hardcover edition as follows:
Names: Phillips, Rowan Ricardo, author.
Title: The circuit : a tennis odyssey / Rowan Ricardo Phillips.
Description: First edition. | New York : Farrar, Straus and Giroux, 2018.
Identifiers: LCCN 2018017728 | ISBN 9780374123772 (hardcover)
Subjects: LCSH: ATP Tour (Organization) | Tennis—Tournaments. |
    Tennis players.
Classification: LCC GV999 .P45 2018 | DDC 796.342—dc23
LC record available at https://lccn.loc.gov/2018017728

Picador Paperback ISBN: 978-1-250-23492-6

Designed by Richard Oriolo

Our books may be purchased in bulk for promotional, educational,
or business use. Please contact your local bookseller or the Macmillan
Corporate and Premium Sales Department at 1-800-221-7945, extension
5442, or by e-mail at MacmillanSpecialMarkets@macmillan.com.

Picador® is a U.S. registered trademark and is used by Macmillan
Publishing Group, LLC, under license from Pan Books Limited.

picadorusa.com • instagram.com/picador
twitter.com/picadorusa • facebook.com/picadorusa

For book club information, please visit facebook.com/picadorbookclub or
e-mail marketing@picadorusa.com.

10 9 8 7 6 5 4 3 2 1

Frontispiece: Photograph (detail) by Ed Lacey / Popperfoto / Getty Images.

For Louisa Thomas

I tell him how the game is organized, the circuit of minor tournaments and the four majors, or Grand Slams, that all players use as yardsticks. I tell him about the tennis calendar, how we start the year on the other side of the world, at the Australian Open, and then just chase the sun.

—ANDRE AGASSI, *Open*

CONTENTS

The court. (Courtesy of the author)

PREFACE

THIS BOOK DOESN'T intend to provide a blow-by-blow account of the entire season of the 2017 ATP Tour. It doesn't cover every tournament. The objective of this book wasn't to report on things for their own sake or out of professional obligation. Other writers do that and some very well. My intention was only to write on what within that year captured my attention repeatedly and in a sustained fashion. For example, Rafa beating everyone senseless on the red clay of Roland-Garros didn't, but the red clay itself did. 2017 was one of the most remarkable years in the history of the ATP Tour. I watched every single match from that year. I don't know how I did it, but I did. I do know why I did it, though. I'd tell you but I'd rather let the tennis tell you.

A BRIEF NOTE ON SCORING

TO CAPTURE THE music, mayhem, and magic of the 2017 season we'll have to go over quite a few final scores and relive scores in the process. If you're familiar with how tennis scoring works, feel free to skip ahead. If you're not and find yourself asking, *What's in a score?*, well, I'm glad you asked.

Tennis scores are depicted in this book in the traditional way. This means many things. Scores in tennis are not simply put in numerical order as they are in baseball, basketball, and many other sports. Those are sports in which the final score is a compilation of the points (or runs), and whoever has the most at the end of the game wins. Tennis is a game in which it's possible to win more points in a match and still lose. Roger Federer has managed to pull off this feat—or have this feat pulled on him—more than twenty times over the course of his career. That's the funny thing about tennis: all points are worth one and only one point but not all points are created equal. Instead, the fate of a tennis

Arthur Ashe (right) celebrating his 6–1, 6–1, 5–7, 6–4 win over Jimmy Connors in the 1975 Wimbledon men's singles final. (Photograph by Ed Lacey / Popperfoto / Getty Images)

match is overwhelmingly decided by moments, and by how players navigate the big points. Therefore, how a scoreline is relayed to others provides a little sense of the ebb and flow of a match. Its very design not only outlines the essential narrative details—who is serving; who is winning; who is losing—but also gives some sense of a match's momentum.

This means that the final score is ordered according to the subject of the sentence. If I write that Player X defeated Player Y by a final score of 6–4, 2–6, 6–1, this means that Player X won the first and third sets 6 games to 4 and 6 games to 1 and lost the second set 2 games to 6. Similarly, if I write that Player Y had lost this same match to Player X, I would write that the final score was 4–6, 6–2, 1–6, with Player Y having lost the first and third sets 4–6, 1–6. Let's pause for a second to make sure we're clear here. While baseball, basketball, and football contests are called games, a tennis game is something different: a tennis game is only a small part of the whole. These numbers you see here represent the number of games each player has won in a given set; each grouping of two numbers—4–6 being one group and 1–6 another—represents a set. Therefore, tennis is a match made up of sets which are made up of games which are made up of points. Most matches are structured so that the player who wins two of three sets wins. Grand Slam matches on the men's tour are best-of-five: the player who wins three sets first wins. A player who wins a Grand Slam match 3–6, 7–5, 1–6, 7–5, 7–5 lost the first and third sets; the player who lost that same match lost it 6–3, 5–7, 6–1, 5–7, 5–7. Look back at the picture on page xii: Arthur Ashe was serving for the match and had double championship point (i.e., two straight chances to win the match and consequently the title). A tennis score is an imperfect storyteller, but it's a storyteller just the same.

Finally, during a game the server's score always goes first: 15–40 means the server has won only one point in this game while the returner won three (this particular score is also known as "double break point"—feel free to consult the glossary that follows for other such terminology). Also, any set showing the score 7–6 indicates that a tiebreaker was played. The number in parentheses next to the 7–6 score reflects the final score of the tiebreaker: 7–6 (11–9), 6–7 (9–11), 7–6 (7–5).

Got it? Good. Here we go down the rabbit hole. Love–love. Don't hold on to anything, things will be better that way.

A GLOSSARY OF TENNIS TERMS

250s: The smallest tournaments on the top circuit are the ATP World Tour 250 tournaments, where the winner is awarded 250 ranking points. Compare this to a Masters 1000 tournament, where the winner is awarded 1,000 ranking points; and a Grand Slam, where the winner is awarded 2,000 points. See *Grand Slam*; *Masters 1000*.

Ace: A serve that, after having landed inside the service box, subsequently makes it past the returner without having been touched by the returner.

Ad court: The left side of the court: the entirety of a tennis court from the center mark to the left. This is the side of the court from which a player serves when the score is advantage, regardless of whose advantage it is. See *Deuce court*.

Advantage: In terms of scoring, the point won immediately after deuce and therefore the point that leaves a player one point from winning the game. Advantage always begins with a serve from the left side of the court. See *Ad court*; *Deuce*; *Game*.

All: In terms of scoring, a synonym for a tied score. When both players have won the same number of points, games, or sets. Said instead of repeating the number: i.e., 15–all is 15–15; 4 games–all in the first set is 4–4 in the first. The exception to this is 40–all, which is referred to as deuce. See *Deuce*.

All-court game: A style of play conducive to grass, clay, and hard court tennis. Implies the player has a well-rounded skill set. An all-court game allows a player to be competitive during all four seasons of the circuit.

Approach shot: A shot hit by a player who intends to follow said shot to the net with the intention of finishing off the point there. Approach shots tend to have a different pace and spin than typical groundstrokes.

ATP: The Association of Tennis Professionals. The principal organizing body of men's professional tennis. Its counterpart for women's professional tennis is the Women's Tennis Association (WTA).

ATP World Tour: The highest circuit of men's professional tennis.

Backcourt: The area of the court between the baseline and the service line.

Backhand: A groundstroke, when the ball is oriented to the non-dominant side of a player, where the back of the stringbed is used to hit the ball. For a right-handed player a backhand would be used to hit a ball from the player's left. For a left-handed player a backhand would be used to hit a ball from the player's right. Originally a one-handed stroke, the two-handed backhand began to rise in popularity with its use in the 1970s by stars such as Björn Borg, Jimmy Connors, and Chris Evert. Now the two-handed backhand is used by the vast majority of professional players. The backhand is often, though by no means always, a player's weaker side and thus the focus of an opponent's tactical approach during a point.

Backspin: The rotation of the tennis ball in the opposite direction of the one in which it's heading, causing the ball to bounce backward when it lands. Slices, chips, and drop shots make pronounced use of backspin.

Balance, stability, focus. Roger Federer's one-handed backhand (*left*) and David Goffin's two-handed backhand (*right*). The Nitto ATP World Tour Finals, London, November 2017. (Photograph of Federer by Clive Brunskill / Getty Images; photograph of Goffin by Julian Finney / Getty Images)

Backswing: The action of drawing back the racket to hit the ball. The initial action of a groundstroke. See *Follow-through*.

Bagel: To be winning or have won no games in a set. Alludes to the shape a bagel shares with the zero on the scoreboard. Often used as a verb. See *Breadstick*.

Ball toss: Also known as a toss, this is the action of the server throwing the ball into the air to begin a serve.

Baseline: At thirty-nine feet, the farthest parallel line from the net on the tennis court. The line from which a player serves. The point of reference by which a player orients herself or himself on the court.

Baseliner: A player whose game is based on playing from the baseline. While it might be inferred that a baseliner is uncomfortable approaching the net, baseliners such as Andy Murray and Rafael Nadal are excellent volleyers as well.

Block: An instinctive and short motion by which a player suddenly places the racket in front of the body in response to a hard shot from the opponent. Usually employed at the net by a player with very little time to react. Also used in the return of serve by players caught by surprise or simply incapable of taking a full swing at the ball. Players with one-handed backhands will often block back hard serves directed to that side of the body.

Breadstick: To be winning or have won only one game in a set. Alludes to the shape a breadstick shares with the number one on the scoreboard. Often used as a verb. See *Bagel*.

Break: To win a game in which the opponent was serving. Often a pivotal moment in the outcome of a set. At the professional level, a break can be a key turn of events, since professionals are expected to protect their service games. Referred to as a "break of serve." To be "up a break": in a set, when a player has one break more than the opponent. To be "down a break": the opposite of being up a break. To be "up a double break": in a set, when a player has two breaks more than the opponent. See *Break point*; *Hold*; *On serve*.

Break point: A point that, if won by the returner, wins the game for the returner. The point prior to any break of serve. For example, 30–40 and advantage for the returner are break-point opportunities. The pendulum on which matches often swing. Scores such as 15–40 and love–40 offer multiple break points in a game, known respectively as "double break point" in the case of 15–40 and "triple break point" in the case of love–40. When a server wins a break point it is referred to as a save. See *Break*; *Hold*.

Buggy whip: The follow-through on a forehand that, instead of crossing the body, returns to the same side of the body from where it began. Think of it as, for a right-handed player, instead of swinging the arm from right to left, rather swinging the arm from right to left and back to the right again with the arm passing over the head as it returns. The shot creates tremendous amounts of topspin. Many of Rafa Nadal's forehands are hit with this style of follow-through. When he wants to hit a flatter ball he follows through across his body instead of using the buggy whip. Roger Federer has used the buggy whip more often in the late stages of his career. See *Backswing*; *Follow-through*.

Bye: An automatic pass into the next round of a tournament. The highest seeds benefit from byes in certain tournaments and therefore don't begin play until the second round. Players at Grand Slam tournaments do not receive byes.

Career Grand Slam: To win all four majors (aka Grand Slam tournaments) over the course of a player's career. Since the beginning of the open era, only five men and six women have achieved this in singles: Rod Laver, Margaret Court, Chris Evert, Martina Navratilova, Steffi Graf, Andre Agassi, Roger Federer, Rafa Nadal, Serena Williams, Maria Sharapova, and Novak Djokovic. See *Grand Slam*.

Carve: To hit a shot with a mixture of spins.

Center mark: The notch in the middle of the baseline. It separates the sides of the court from which a player must serve on any given point.

Challenge: When a player appeals to the chair umpire over a line call and Hawk-Eye camera technology is used to review the appeal. A player receives three challenges per set and an additional challenge if the set extends to a tiebreak. Not all tournaments have Hawk-Eye technology and not all courts at a tournament that uses Hawk-Eye technology may have Hawk-Eye technology available. The clay court tournaments still opt for a physical spot check by the chair umpire, who descends to the court to inspect the mark left by the ball in the clay when questionable calls arise. See *Line call*; *Line judge*.

Championship point: Match point of a tournament final. See *Match point*.

Changeover: The ninety-second period during which players can sit, rest, and refresh themselves prior to switching sides of the court. This occurs after each odd-number game. A changeover between sets lasts slightly longer: 120 seconds.

Chip: To hit a low shot with backspin, often deployed as an approach shot.

Chip and charge: A tactic by which a player hits a chip shot and rushes to the net behind it.

Clay: One of the three main playing surfaces of tennis, and the slowest. Made of numerous crushed materials, including brick, clay, shale, and stone. The visible top layer makes up only a small percentage of the surface. Clay is famed for its reddish-orange color but professional tournaments have also used green, blue, and gray. Due to the processes required to produce these changes in hue, different colors affect the bounce of the ball. The slow-playing surface also causes the ball to bounce higher than it does on the other surfaces and as a result tends to extend game play, which is beneficial to grinders and baseliners while detrimental to serve-and-volleyers. Because the clay surface gives, sliding is an effective technique in game play both for reaching the ball and conserving energy. Overall, the surface rewards players with excellent footwork. Conversely, it tends to hinder more cumbersome players. See *Grass; Hard court.*

Closed stance: Regarding foot positioning, hitting a groundstroke with the front foot crossed in front of the back foot, leaving the shoulder facing the net. This was classic groundstroke technique until balls started being hit with so much pace that using this footwork was impractical, as it robbed time (and angles) from the player. See *Open stance.*

Code violation: As observed by the ATP and WTA, a penalty for a rule violation generally in regard to on-court decorum and protocol. Examples include smashing a racket, uttering an obscenity, smashing balls into the stands during the match, inappropriate clothing, using a cell phone, communicating with one's coach, etc. Code violations escalate in penalty: the first violation results in a warning to the player in violation; the second results in a point penalty; the third in a game penalty; and the fourth in forfeiture of the match.

Crosscourt: A shot that travels from the ad court to the deuce court or vice versa. See *Ad court*; *Deuce court*; *Down the line*.

Davis Cup: Annual international men's team competition in which countries compete in staggered single-elimination events throughout the year. The Davis Cup is organized by the International Tennis Federation (ITF) and not the ATP.

Deuce: In terms of scoring, after 40–all, when both players have the same number of points in a game. When the player who has advantage in a game loses the next point, the score returns to deuce. See *Advantage*; *Game*.

Deuce court: The right side of the court: all of the court from the center mark to the right. This is the side of the court where a player serves when the score is deuce. See *Ad court*.

Dirtballer: A clay court specialist. Not quite as pejorative as it sounds. The term "dirt rat" is also common. While it means the same thing as "dirtballer"—a player whose success is almost exclusively on clay courts—"dirt rat" is a more pejorative term.

Double break point: See *Break point*.

Double fault: Missing the service box on both opportunities to serve, resulting in the loss of a point. The ultimate unforced error.

Doubles alley: The space on the court between the singles and doubles sideline.

Down the line: In singles, a shot that runs parallel to the singles line. In doubles, a shot that runs parallel to the doubles line. I was tempted to describe it as a straight shot, but players have become adept at hitting "banana shots" by striking the outside of the ball in such a way that the ball arcs out and then curves back in to catch the sideline.

Draw: The arrangement and sequence of matches, from round to round, in any tournament as organized by a combination of seeding and random selection. Tournaments have qualifying rounds prior to the official tournament for lower-ranked players from which players enter the main draw as qualifiers. A select few wild cards are also given entry at the discretion of the tournament organizers. Qualifiers and wild cards are usually unseeded, the exception being a high-ranked player who is granted wild-card entry into a tournament. For example, when Novak Djokovic joined the draw of the 2017 Aegon International in Eastbourne, England, late as a wild card in order to tune up for Wimbledon, he was seeded first. The better a player's seeding, the better, theoretically, his or her draw. Only the first round of a draw is known at the start of a tournament, although possible opponents in the succeeding rounds can then be deduced by the structure of the sections of the draw. There are different sizes of draws depending on the tournament. All Grand Slams are 128-draw tournaments. Others include 64-draw tournaments, 56-draw tournaments, and 32-draw tournaments. See *Qualifier*; *Round of sixteen*; *Seeding*; *Wild card*.

Drop shot: A shot that falls to the court just after having crossed the net. The closer to the net it falls, the better the drop shot. Typically utilized as a tactical surprise against a player standing far behind the baseline. Also regularly the fallback option of a struggling player short on ideas or fitness. Either way, used with the intent to end a point or draw an opponent to the net in order to hit a passing shot. See *Passing shot*.

Drop volley: A drop shot hit from a position near the net.

Error: A shot that lands outside the opponent's court or into the net.

Exhibition: A match or tournament primarily for entertainment purposes. No ranking points are involved.

Fault: The same as an error but off the serve as opposed to during a point. Players get one freebie per serve. See *Double fault*; *Second serve*.

Fed Cup: Annual international women's team competition in which countries compete in staggered single-elimination events throughout the year. The Fed Cup is organized by the International Tennis Federation (ITF) and not the WTA.

First serve: The most important shot in tennis. The initial attempt by a player to serve successfully into the opponent's service box. The first serve tends to be more aggressive in pace, placement, and strategy because the server has a second opportunity if needed.

Flat: A shot typically hit hard and without much spin. Called flat because of its trajectory over the net.

Follow-through: The opposite of backswing. The final part of the motion of a player's swing pattern. See *Backswing*; *Buggy whip*.

Futures: The third rung of circuits in men's tennis below the Challenger Tour and the ATP World Tour. Players on the Futures circuit attempt to accumulate enough ranking points to qualify for Challenger Tour events. As its name implies, the Futures circuit ideally is for younger players seeking to gain experience and ranking points as they develop. Nevertheless, this isn't really the case, as many longtime professionals with low rankings compete at this level.

Game: The basic unit of a set. One player serves during its duration, which lasts as long as necessary to see it to completion. A game may last thirty seconds or shorter. A game may last thirty minutes or longer. The points in a game are counted as follows: love, 15, 30, 40, deuce (if necessary), advantage (if necessary). A player must win a game by two points. This is why if a game goes to 40–all, or deuce, one player must score advantage and then one more point to win the game. If only one player in a game arrives to 40—be it 40–30, 40–15, or 40–love—then the game can be won if that player wins the next point. This moment is referred to as game point. See *Advantage*; *Deuce*; *Game point*; *Set*.

Game point: When a player is one point away from winning a game. See *Advantage*; *Deuce*; *Set*.

Ghost into the net: A tactic. When a player subtly and unexpectedly approaches the net when the opponent is otherwise distracted with playing the ball.

Grand Slam: Until recently, winning all four major tournaments—the Australian Open, the French Open, Wimbledon, and the U.S. Open—in the same calendar year. Now each of these tournaments, once known as majors, are widely referred to colloquially and officially as Grand Slams. See *Career Grand Slam*.

Grass: One of the three main playing surfaces of tennis and the least common. Generally the fastest court surface, which produces the lowest-bouncing ball. A boon to players who prefer short points, as the speed and low trajectory of the ball during play on grass produces far fewer rallies than clay and hard court surfaces do. Beneficial to big servers and detrimental to players with large backswings that take away from the response time of their groundstrokes. The kindest part of the circuit to serve-and-volleyers. That said, due to a change in the type of grass seed used to the more rapid-drying 100 percent ryegrass, the courts at Wimbledon now produce a higher-bouncing ball and consequently play slower than they did in years past.

Grinder: A player whose principal strategy is to repeatedly play out long rallies from the baseline in the hopes of wearing down the opponent. This tactic has been encouraged by slower court surfaces, increased physical endurance, and improved racket equipment.

Grip: Two meanings—how a player holds the racket, which affects swing path and shot production; also, the exterior wrap of the racket handle.

Groundie: Slang for groundstroke.

Groundstroke: A swung forehand or backhand hit after the ball has bounced.

Half volley: A groundstroke or volley struck immediately after the ball bounces on the court.

Hard court: One of the three main playing surfaces of tennis, typically made of asphalt or concrete with a synthetic top layer. Courts can be produced for a large variety of playing speeds. Hard courts were originally fast by design, but technology has seen them evolve to occupy a number of speeds as of late, ranging from extremely fast to nearly clay-court-paced. Therefore, one can't assume a court is fast because it's a hard court. Indian Wells and Miami are renowned for being slow hard courts, the latter being a notoriously extreme example, while Shanghai is known for being a fast hard court. After a general trend of slowing down hard courts over the years, the organizers of the Australian Open took to speeding up their hard courts for the 2017 edition of the tournament. The results speak for themselves.

Head: The part of the racket above the neck that frames the stringbed.

Hold: When the player who is serving wins the game. The opposite of a break. Commonly referred to as to hold serve. See *Break*; *On serve*.

Inside-in forehand: When a player hits a forehand from the ad court to the opponent's deuce court. In other words, when a ball is hit to the backhand side of a player's court and the player hits a forehand from that backhand position directly down the line. Also known as running around the backhand. See *Down the line*; *Inside-out forehand*.

Inside-out backhand: When a player, in this case right-handed, hits a backhand from the deuce court to the opponent's deuce court. In other words, when a ball is hit to the forehand side of a player's court and the player hits a backhand from that forehand position diagonally across the court. Less frequently seen than the inside-out forehand. See *Inside-out forehand*.

Inside-out forehand: When a player, again in this case right-handed, hits a forehand from the ad court to the opponent's ad court. In other words, when a ball is on the backhand side of a player's court and the player hits a forehand from that backhand position diagonally across the court. Also known as running around the backhand. See *Inside-out backhand*.

ITF: The International Tennis Federation. In charge of the Davis Cup, the Fed Cup, and Olympic tennis, among other events. A separate entity from the men's ATP and the women's WTA.

Junk ball: A type of shot with little in the way of reliable spin, pace, or distance. Used to disrupt the rhythm of the opponent. Very few top players hit junk balls.

Kick serve: A serve hit with sufficient spin to bounce high and discomfit the returner.

Let: When a point must be replayed. Most commonly when a serve hits the net cord and nevertheless lands within the service box. A serve is not valid if it touches the net; that said, when such a serve lands inside the service box the server is given an opportunity to repeat the serve. If the let occurs on the first serve, then the server will repeat the first serve; if the let occurs on the second serve, then the server will repeat the second serve. For this reason, the chair umpire will announce, "Let: first serve" or "Let: second serve." In this situation, there is no limit to the number of lets a server can be granted. Lets are not solely related to the net, however. Any number of in-game distractions can cause a let—from distracting court noise to something straying onto the court—and thus a replay of the point.

Line call: The determination made by a line judge of whether a ball landed inside or outside the court. A call of out is made vocally, a call of in is made via hand signals. A line call can be reviewed by a player's challenge. See *Challenge*.

Line judge: Part of the officiating team placed at strategic places on the court to observe and confirm whether a ball is in or out. Balls that are out are announced with the call "Out," while balls that are in are silently indicated by pointing at the ground with arms extended and palms down. See *Challenge*; *Line call*.

Main draw: The actual tournament, after qualifying has concluded. See *Draw*.

Masters 1000s: Known officially as the ATP World Tour Masters 1000 tournaments. A series of nine prestigious tournaments spread throughout the calendar year that award 1,000 ranking points to the winner, 600 points to the defeated finalist, 360 points to the semifinalist, etc. Grand Slam tournaments are worth 2,000 points for the winner, 1,200 points for the finalist, etc. Aside from Grand Slams, only the ATP Tour Finals awards more points (1,500 for the winner, etc.) than Masters 1000 tournaments. The nine take place, based on their order on the calendar, in the following locales: Indian Wells (Palm Springs); Key Biscayne (Miami); Monte Carlo; Madrid; Rome; Montreal/Toronto; Mason, Ohio (Cincinnati); Shanghai; and Paris. See *250s*; *Grand Slam*.

Match point: The moment when a player is one point away from winning the match. Similarly, set point is when a player is one point away from winning the set. Championship point is when a player is one point away from winning the tournament.

Mishit: When the ball is struck by a part of the racket that is not the sweet spot of the stringbed, causing the ball to take off on an unintended trajectory. See *Shank*.

Moonball: A slow topspin groundstroke that crosses the net at an extreme height.

Net cord: When the ball inadvertently hits the upper cord of the net in the middle of a rally. This can be an unexpected benefit or hindrance to either player in the point.

No-man's-land: During a point, the area of the court between the baseline and the service line. As the name suggests, one of the worst places to position oneself on the court.

On serve: The score of a set when neither player is up a break. If the score of a set is 4–3 on serve, this means that the player who has won three games is about to serve; therefore, that player has the opportunity to tie the set. If this player subsequently holds, the score is then 4–all on serve. On serve does not mean that there have been no breaks in a set—the term only describes the current state of the set: that there have been an equal number of breaks of serve, whether that number is four or zero. See *Break*; *Hold*.

Open: An open is a tennis tournament that is open to both professionals and amateurs. This does not mean that open tournaments are open to all and sundry. These tournaments have eligibility requirements. A player needs a sufficiently high ranking to enter the main draw of an ATP open tournament directly. The same holds true for the preliminary qualifying rounds of these tournaments. See *Draw*; *Qualifier*; *Open era*.

Open era: Beginning in 1968, when tennis tournaments became open to both professional and amateur players. The unofficial mark that separates one era of tennis from the other.

Open stance: Regarding foot positioning, hitting a groundstroke while the body is facing the net. A general practice now of professional players on the forehand side. Less so on the backhand side, but some of the best backhands in the game, such as those of Serena Williams and Novak Djokovic, are often hit with an open stance. This is far less common with one-handed backhands, but Stan Wawrinka and Dominic Thiem are highly proficient at it.

Overhead: Excluding the serve, hitting a ball that is arm's length above the head or higher. When hit with assertive force, commonly referred to as an overhead smash.

Passing shot: A shot that goes by a player who has moved up the court.

Platform stance: Positioning the feet during the serve with one foot slightly ahead of the other and not moving them from that position during the service motion until the ball is struck. As opposed to a pinpoint stance, during which a player brings the feet together at the baseline in the middle of the service motion.

Qualifier: A player who is made eligible for the main draw of a tournament by having participated in the rounds of qualification that preceded it.

Rally: During a point, the exchange of a number of shots for a noticeable duration of time.

Retire: When a player is unable to continue in a match due to injury or illness and therefore forfeits the match. When a player retires prior to the beginning of the match, this is known as a walkover.

Return: The first shot made by the receiver in response to the serve.

Round of sixteen: Refers to when sixteen players are left in a tournament. What point in the tournament this is depends on the number of players in the draw. In a Grand Slam tournament the round of sixteen is the fourth round. In a 56-draw tournament (for instance, Monte Carlo and Shanghai), the round of sixteen is the third round.

Scoreline: The score of a match in process or the final result of a match.

Second serve: If the server misses the first opportunity to serve the ball correctly into the opponent's court, this is the second and final opportunity for the server to do so. Missing the second serve results in a double fault, gifting a free point to the opponent. Therefore, the overwhelming priority of the second serve is to land the ball inside the service box. For this reason, the second serve tends to be safer. However, hitting a safer serve without care for placement, speed, and spin gives the opponent free license to tee off on the serve, thereby putting the server immediately on the defensive and robbing him or her of any initiative—an initiative that is the sole benefit of serving in the first place. The second serve is the secret battleground of any tennis match. The better a player's second serve, the more success is likely to come on the circuit. Andy Murray and Novak Djokovic in particular became players of an entirely other level once they improved their second serves. Meanwhile, Pete Sampras passed on the idea of changing his serve altogether on the second serve: he hit two first serves instead. A handful of current players have tried emulating this tactic, to mixed results. See *Double fault*; *First serve*; *Let*.

Seed: The number by which a player is positioned in a tournament draw. The higher a player's seed, the further away from other high seeds the player is arranged within the draw. The size of the draw determines the number of seeds. A player's seed is largely, although not exclusively, based on the ranking of the player; past performance of the player at the tournament also factors into a player's seeding by tournament officials. For example, entering the 2014 Wimbledon Championships Rafa Nadal was the number-one-ranked player in the world, Novak Djokovic was ranked second, Stan Wawrinka third, Roger Federer fourth, and Andy Murray fifth. And yet, Djokovic was seeded first, Nadal was seeded second, Murray was seeded third, Federer fourth, and Wawrinka fifth. (I know you're curious: Djokovic ended up defeating Federer in a five-set final.) See *Draw*; *Round of sixteen*.

Serve-and-volley: An offensive tactic of long-standing practice, now far less common, in which a player rushes to the net following the serve. Designed to end the point quickly by cutting off the angles of the returner, thereby pressuring the opponent into hitting an error or a sitter. Improvements to racket technology and increasingly slower court speeds have combined to undermine the effectiveness of this tactic. This in turn has depleted the number of expert volleyers on the tour. Still, the serve-and-volley was the preeminent tactic of championship tennis for generations. Practitioners included Arthur Ashe, Rod Laver, Stan Smith (yes, that Stan Smith), Martina Navratilova, John McEnroe, and Stefan Edberg. Countered by the emergence of elite baseliners beginning in the 1970s, such as Chris Evert, Jimmy Connors, Björn Borg, and Ivan Lendl. In the family tree of tennis styles, Federer is from the branch of the serve-and-volleyers, while Rafa Nadal, Andy Murray, and Novak Djokovic are from the branch of the baseliners. To date, the Sampras-Agassi rivalry marked the last time a pure serve-and-volleyer and a pure baseline player routinely competed in finals on the men's circuit. The paucity of serve-and-volley in today's game can make it an effective surprise tactic during a given moment in a point or for the duration of the match. For the latter, see Andy Murray vs. Mischa Zverev, 2017 Australian Open, round of sixteen. See *Baseline*; *Baseliner*; *Grass*; *Grinder*.

Service box: The two rectangular areas of the court between the net and the service line portioned off by the centerline of the court and the singles sideline. The area inside where the server must place the ball without touching the net in order to start the point.

Set: The largest unit of scoring in a match. A set is the container in which games are counted and by which matches are divided. Grand Slam matches on the men's circuit are best-of-five sets, as are Davis Cup matches. All other matches are best-of-three (although they used to be best-of-five as well). All matches on the women's tour are best-of-three. The requisite number of games to win a set is as follows: six, provided the opponent has won four or less; or seven if the opponent has won five. If the score of a set arrives at 6–all, a tiebreak is usually then played in order to decide the winner of the set. See *Game*; *Tiebreak*.

Shank: A mishit ball, often off the frame of the racket. Not at all indicative of a professional player's ability but rather of swing path, court positioning, and intent of the shot: Roger Federer shanks more balls than anyone on the circuit. See *Mishit*.

Singles: A match with only two players. A tournament of singles matches.

Sitter: A shot that poses, or at least should pose, no difficulty for the opposing player to put away for a winner.

Split step: A learned, automated motion of a player preparing to react to a ball hit by the opponent. It consists of a slight hop and separation of the feet to shoulder-width distance while remaining centrally balanced on the balls of the feet. Intended to prepare the player to react quickly in any direction.

Straight sets: To win a match without losing a set.

Stringbed: The perpendicular crosshatch of tensed strings threaded through the oval frame of the racket head.

The T: Where the centerline and service line on a tennis court meet, forming a T on the court.

Tiebreak: Played at the end of a set that has ended with both players having won six games apiece (6–all). The winner is the first to arrive at seven points or win by two points, whichever comes first. Unlike a normal game, in a tiebreak the player who serves first gets only one serve, after which the players alternate serve

Milos Raonic in trophy position. Roland-Garros, Paris, France, June 2017.
(Photograph by Martin Sidorják)

every two points. When a player wins a point on the opponent's serve it's known as a mini-break.

Topspin: When the ball spins in the same direction in which it's traveling. This causes the ball to dip quickly either just past the net or just before reaching the baseline, depending on the depth of the shot. Topspin also entices the ball to bounce off the court at a higher angle. Racket and string innovations have led to an exponentially greater use of topspin in the game.

Triple break point: See *Break point*.

Trophy position: The part of the service motion when the ball has been tossed into the air, the server's arm that tossed the ball is still straight, and the arm with the racket is bent behind the body. The service motion of a player is idiosyncratic, but all players pass through trophy position at some moment in the service motion. Derives its name from being the typical pose used for tennis trophies.

Tweener: A trick shot hit while the ball is between the legs. Two variations exist. The classic one involves running back from the net toward the baseline to chase down a lob and, instead of spinning to hit the ball back across the net, the player attempts to hit the ball between the legs while still running back toward the baseline. Brought into fashion by Guillermo Villas in the 1970s, who dubbed the shot the Gran Willy. The later version involves, while standing in normal ready position, hitting the ball between the legs during a normal rally for absolutely no reason at all, as both Gaël Monfils and Nick Kyrgios have on occasion.

Unforced error: An error made by a player that is not due to anything the opponent did during the point. For instance, hitting a sitter into the net or sending an easy forehand far over the baseline would be considered unforced errors.

Unseeded player: An entrant into a tournament who is not a seeded player, a qualifier, or a wild card. Unseeded players navigate the no-man's-land of a draw where they can be pitted against any type of player in the first round of the tournament. That said, this is still better than being a qualifier because the unseeded player hasn't expended physical and emotional energy playing qualifying matches.

Volley: A shot hit before the ball bounces, usually but not exclusively while the player is near the net. Different from a groundstroke, a volley typically has neither backswing nor follow-through. An increasing number of players are making use of a swinging volley, which is when a player takes a full swing at the ball before it lands in the court. Players who are strongly associated with the swinging volley include Andre Agassi, Maria Sharapova, Serena and Venus Williams, and Novak Djokovic.

Walkover: A player's uncontested victory due to the opponent's inability to begin the match; usually, although not exclusively, due to injury. See *Retire*.

Wild card: A player invited directly into the main draw of a tournament. Reasons for a wild card vary. Sometimes wild-card invitations are given to promising young talents from the country in which the tournament is held to provide them with early opportunities in ATP events that they otherwise would not have had. In a similar vein, some tournaments offer wild cards to young foreign talents as acts of reciprocity. Some wild cards are given to players who are only recently returning from injury and therefore do not have the requisite ranking points to qualify for direct entry but whose presence the organizers believe will benefit the tournament as a whole. And sometimes a top player decides late to participate in an upcoming tournament for one reason or another and, if the tournament has reserved a wild card, it will be extended to the player.

Winner: A shot that lands inside the opponent's court and that the opponent does not reach, and that by consequence wins the point for the player.

WTA: The Women's Tennis Association. The principal organizing body of women's professional tennis. Its counterpart for men's professional tennis is the Association of Tennis Professionals (ATP).

Ready . . . Play

WIMBLEDON

The 2017 Wimbledon Championships began on the third of July. The day prior, the President of the United States sent out via Twitter an edited video image of himself delivering a staged beating of former wrestling executive Vince McMahon on the outskirts of a ring, with the logo of the cable news network CNN superimposed over where McMahon's head belonged; and the then-governor of New Jersey, Chris Christie, was photographed in a bathing suit, baseball cap, and T-shirt enjoying a lovely summer Sunday with his family on the beach of a state park that, like all of them, he had shut down due to a budget impasse. Independence Day in America was a day away, and luckily I was far away. I turned on the television set.

I was in the mountains, not far from towns with names like La Nou de Gaià, Masllorenç, Salomó, and Tamarit, where all the vertigo-inducing, winding roads lead downhill first to Torre-dembarra and on to Tarragona. Another summer in Catalonia:

north of Barcelona, south of Barcelona, a few scattered weeks of Barcelona in between.

Here is where, year after year, Wimbledon happens for me.

This also means that my Wimbledon has been seen through the lens of this place, my second home, for a good chunk of my life. For instance, every year during the thirteen days of the tournament, some 150,000 servings of the fabled fresh strawberries from Kent County, England, partnered with generous helpings of sweet clotted cream, are consumed on the Wimbledon grounds. It's as iconic as Cracker Jacks and hot dogs at a baseball game and mint juleps at Churchill Downs. And every year the Spanish television network goes through the trouble of having a correspondent who is covering the tournament try the dish live on the air just to point out that the strawberries, though good, can't hold a candle to the strawberries grown in Huelva, where 96 percent of the 250,000 tons of strawberries produced annually in Spain are grown, making it the second largest source of strawberries in the world as well as the biggest exporter of them on the planet.

You can imagine what being here for the 2008 Wimbledon final was like. Often referred to as the greatest tennis match of all time—though I'm not buying it—this final was the moment when the Federer-Nadal rivalry became something greater than a rivalry: it became a notch on the cultural time line. It played out over four hours and forty-eight minutes—6–4, 6–4, 6–7 (5–7), 6–7 (8–10), 9–7—extending so late into the day that a visible darkness descended ominously over Centre Court. The points played long, with Rafa constantly escaping near-death situations by retrieving balls that looked certain to get past him and using his lefty-spin serve in do-or-die moments to live to see another point. I'll never forget the numerous, varied, and unreserved nervous breakdowns of the Spanish broadcasting team, who, unlike their American and English counterparts, never bother with any silly charade of impartiality when it comes to important matters such as these.

After having lost two straight Wimbledon finals to Roger Federer, Rafael Nadal, known as Rafa, won, and in the process broke a string of five straight titles at the tournament for Federer. It seemed at the time like one of those self-contained victories, a bauble, a blip, a skip of the record: Nadal showed the world that he was much more than a clay-court specialist and, in defeating Federer at his most cherished venue, that he was more than a muscle-shirt-wearing impediment to Federer's historical legacy. He was that afternoon at Wimbledon a harbinger of change. For, although Federer would take the title back the following year and win it again in 2012, all of the other Wimbledons from 2008 to 2016 were won by Nadal, Novak Djokovic, or Andy Murray, players who are variations on a theme of a similar style far removed from the classic serve-and-volley tactics that are the roots from which both Federer and Wimbledon itself have flourished. The sea change after Nadal's 2008 win was so sudden, strong, and convincing that Federer's 2012 Wimbledon victory, a mere four years later, was generally greeted with surprise.

When the 2017 tennis season started, the aftershocks of Nadal's intervention in 2008 were still being felt on the Wimbledon grass. Nadal himself couldn't sustain the brief success he had enjoyed on the surface, but both Djokovic and Murray continued to carry the torch there for the defensive baseliners. Despite game resistance from Federer in the 2014 and 2015 Wimbledon finals, Djokovic's wins felt like a fait accompli. As did Murray's 2016 title against big-serving Milos Raonic.

In Rafa's absence, the Spanish broadcasts focus on strategy and technique, they intone on the history of head-to-head matchups, recent performances, and how these may affect a player's psychology at a high or low moment in the match. The forehand is "the right" (or, for the English, "the drive"), whether you use your right or left, whether you're conservative or liberal; and the backhand is "the other side" and the same word for "setback," "misfortune," or "hitch"—as early as 2004 you'd hear the intrepid suggestion that a player who could repeatedly successfully attack Federer's backhand would be able to knock him off his perch. The story behind Federer's return to dominance in 2017 was his ability and, it has to be said, his willingness to finally figure that out.

Summer 2017. Half the year gone, and where were we? Federer sweeping away all before him on the hard-court swing of the first quarter of the circuit, Nadal not far behind. Then, during the second quarter of the year, the clay-court swing, Federer takes a pass and Nadal does the same. Except for Rome, where he lost in the quarterfinals to one emergent talent, the powerful Dominic Thiem, and saw Sascha Zverev beat Djokovic in the final to become the youngest player since Djokovic to win a Masters 1000 title. Was it Zverev's time now? Were the young legs of the tour gaining strength as the circuit approached summer? Was winter and spring's fountain of youth drying up? Was it in the cards for Zverev to be a threat at Wimbledon? His record thus far in Grand Slams was abysmal, and he followed up the biggest win of his career in Rome by losing in the first round in Paris to the thirty-three-year-old Fernando Verdasco. So probably not.

The grass-court season weighs heavy on the imagination of the tennis lover, but it's a blip on the circuit: the middle of June to the middle of July, three concurrent pairs of 250- and 500-level tournaments—'s-Hertogenbosch and Stuttgart, Halle and the Queen's Club in London, then Eastbourne and Antalya—all serving as summer warm-ups for Wimbledon. Most players tend to play two tournaments in the grass-court season: one of those six grass warm-ups and then the big one, Wimbledon. Some of the Americans and big-servers tack on a third by signing up for the one grass-court tournament after Wimbledon, the Hall of Fame ceremonial tournament in Newport, Rhode Island. All of this is to say that Wimbledon is a tournament that sneaks up on you. Unlike the French and U.S. Opens, there aren't a bevy of big similar-surfaced tournaments leading up to it. In the past twenty years only seven men have won it. To put this in proper perspective, despite Nadal having won ten titles in Paris, ten men have won the French Open in the past twenty years. So who was the favorite coming into Wimbledon? Federer was just starting to play again, and besides, how could he keep up that pace? Nadal was the hottest player on the circuit, but it seemed wistful to think he'd win Wimbledon, considering he'd only made it out of the second round of the tournament once since 2012. Was it then the top-seeded, still-top-ranked and defending Murray, who had thus far been struggling all year to find the best form? Was it Djokovic, who had just won the warm-up in Eastbourne and was returning to the site where his 2016 season went from glorious to ungainly and mysteriously fell off the hinges?

That Wimbledon was the strangest I'd ever seen and the most important one in my life. I remember thinking how strange it was to be listening to match commentary in English. It had been so long. And it made the game feel like it was being played in a different dimension. I lived in a Wimbledon haze; every match seemed like a green thought in a green shade, and I couldn't walk or feel my leg.

I spent Wimbledon 2016 alone in New York, living on the sofa. My left leg was a lamppost: it was wrapped in a soft cast and numerous spools of gauze in order to protect the threads and staples holding together the frayed halves of my Achilles tendon, which had snapped and left both my leg and my summer dead.

They say that when you tear your Achilles it feels like you've been shot in the back of the leg or jabbed by a knife. But it wasn't like that. I was playing basketball—the wrong sport at the wrong time—and it just went, simple as that. It was more as though the tendon were a venetian blind being opened quickly, harshly, the way you do it when you want to wake someone up. I'd never really been injured before. I asked my surgeon if I could have done anything to prevent it. He said, *Be younger. I'm only forty-one*, I said. *Exactly*, he said. I sighed.

The 2016 Wimbledon Championships started the day before I went under. I remember watching the American Sam Querrey beat the Czech Lukáš Rosol in an absolute thriller—12–10 in the fifth—and thinking he couldn't ask for more excitement at Wimbledon than that. Of course, he was destined to defeat Djokovic in the third round (over three days!) and snap the Serb's remarkable thirty-match Grand Slam winning streak.

Along with every other match at that Wimbledon, I watched both of those Querrey matches thrice in their entirety. I had nowhere to go and no way of getting there. So I lived in stasis on the sofa with Wimbledon on live and Wimbledon on replay, day into night and night into day, with an endless glass of lemonade, four pillows to prop up my leg, and a bottomless prescription of oxycodone with instructions to take a dose every few hours or, you know, simply when it felt like some pain was on the way. Admittedly, this is a very messed-up way to watch Wimbledon. Nevertheless, that's how I took it all in: the tense Serena-Kerber women's final, Federer's fall (literally and figuratively) in the men's semis, Murray making the most of his chance to consolidate his status with a second title, and the beginning of Djokovic's strange wane. I watched them all three times. There was also a reconnection with a part of me I didn't even know I had lost. I used to watch tennis all the time—just without the devastating injury, abject loneliness, and highly addictive painkillers. I used to get up at all kinds of absurd hours for matches and record them on VHS and then record over those when I didn't have any more VHS tapes. I used to hit tennis balls against a handball wall, against a metal gate, simply into the distance—whatever it would take to have a racket in my hand. Tennis was the one sport my parents and I would watch together. My father would actually suggest this—*Hey, Agassi-Edberg is about to start, let's watch it*—which I had forgotten. I had forgotten it all. I don't know how or why, but tennis slowly became a private joy. I kept watching, by myself. I stopped playing. I never competed. I'm not very competitive. Now I spend hours hitting with my friends. When we play points we rarely keep score. At some point that private joy became something I wanted to share again, and so when my leg was good enough to handle the strain I started to play again. And even before that I knew I wanted to write it out, have an experience in words, which is the best and most genuine way I can think of sharing. Wimbledon was at the middle of all of this. I smelled the grass, and I saw on the flatscreen thousands of shades of green.

Regardless of the outcome, Wimbledon 2017 was already different. Not only had tennis done something strange—both change by going forward and change by going back—but so had I. Back in the mountains, not far from towns with names like La Nou de Gaià, Masllorenç, Salomó, and Tamarit, where all the vertigo-inducing, winding roads lead downhill first to Torredembarra and then to Tarragona, it was a half hour past noon. I looked over the schedule of play to see what matches were set to start the tournament off—Jo-Wilfried Tsonga vs. Cameron Norrie; Pierre-Hugues Herbert vs. Nick Kyrgios; Camila Giorgi vs. Alizé Cornet; Sam Querrey vs. Thomas Fabbiano; Dustin Brown vs. João Sousa—and then I picked one. And bided my time.

THE CALENDAR

WK	START DATE	CITY	CURRENT TOURNAMENT NAME	SURFACE	DRAW	PRIZE MONEY
1	Jan 1	Brisbane	Brisbane International presented by Suncorp	H	28	$437,380
	Jan 2	Doha	Qatar ExxonMobil Open	H	32	$1,237,190
	Jan 2	Chennai	Aircel Chennai Open	H	28	$447,480
2	Jan 8	Sydney	Apia International Sydney	H	28	$437,280
	Jan 9	Auckland	ASB Classic	H	28	$450,110
3	Jan 16	Melbourne	Australian Open	H	128	$2,665,000
4						
5						
6	Feb 6	Montpellier	Open Sud de France	IH	28	$482,060
	Feb 6	Sofia	Garanti Koza Sofia Open	IH	28	$482,060
	Feb 6	Quito	Ecuador Open Quito	CL	28	$482,060
7	Feb 13	Rotterdam	ABN AMRO World Tennis Tournament	IH	32	$1,724,930
	Feb 13	Memphis	Memphis Open	IH	28	$642,750
	Feb 13	Buenos Aires	Argentina Open	CL	28	$546,680
8	Feb 20	Rio de Janeiro	Rio Open presented by Claro	CL	32	$1,461,560
	Feb 20	Marseille	Open 13 Provence	IH	28	€620,660
	Feb 20	Delray Beach	Delray Beach Open	H	32	$534,625
9	Feb 27	Dubai	Dubai Duty Free Tennis Championships	H	32	$2,429,150
	Feb 27	Acapulco	Abierto Mexicano Telcel	H	32	$1,491,310
	Feb 27	São Paulo	Brasil Open	CL	28	$455,565
10	Mar 9	Indian Wells	BNP Paribas Open	H	96	$6,993,450
11						
12	Mar 22	Miami	Miami Open presented by Itau	H	96	$6,993,450
13						

H = Hard court
G = Grass court
CL = Clay court
IH = Indoor Hard

WK	START DATE	CITY	CURRENT TOURNAMENT NAME	SURFACE	DRAW	PRIZE MONEY
14						
15	Apr 10	Houston	Fayez Sarofim & Co. Men's Clay Court Championship	CL	28	$535,625
	Apr 10	Marrakech	Grand Prix Hassan II	CL	28	€482,060
16	Apr 15	Monte Carlo	Monte Carlo Rolex Masters	CL	56	€4,273,775
17	Apr 24	Barcelona	Barcelona Open BancSabadell	CL	48	€2,324,905
	Apr 24	Budapest	Hungarian Open	CL	28	€482,060
18	May 1	Estoril	Millennium Estoril Open	CL	28	€482,060
	May 1	Munich	BMW Open by FWU AG	CL	28	€482,060
	May 1	Istanbul	TEB BNP Paribas Istanbul Open	CL	28	€439,005
19	May 7	Madrid	Mutua Madrid Open	CL	56	€5,439,350
20	May 14	Rome	Internazionali BNL d'Italia	CL	56	€4,273,775
21	May 21	Geneva	Banque Eric Sturdza Geneva Open	CL	28	€482,060
	May 21	Lyon	Open Parc Auvergne-Rhône-Alpes Lyon	CL	28	€482,060
22	May 28	Paris	Roland-Garros	CL	128	€2,200,000
23						
24	Jun 12	's-Hertogen-bosch	Ricoh Open	G	28	€589,185
	Jun 12	Stuttgart	Mercedes Cup	G	28	€630,785
25	Jun 19	Halle	Gerry Weber Open	G	32	€1,836,660
	Jun 19	London	Aegon Championships	G	32	€1,836,660
26	Jun 25	Eastbourne	Aegon International	G	28	€635,660
	Jun 25	Antalya	Antalya Cup	G	28	€439,005
27	July 3	London	Wimbledon Championship	G	128	€2,504,480
28						
29	Jul 17	Newport	Hall of Fame Tennis Championships	G	28	$535,625
	Jul 17	Båstad	SkiStar Swedish Open	CL	28	€482,060
	Jul 17	Umag	Konzum Croatia Open Umag	CL	28	€482,060

WK	START DATE	CITY	CURRENT TOURNAMENT NAME	SURFACE	DRAW	PRIZE MONEY
30	Jul 24	Hamburg	German Tennis Championships	CL	32	€1,499,940
	Jul 24	Atlanta	BB&T Atlanta Open	H	28	$642,750
	Jul 24	Gstaad	J. Safra Sarasin Swiss Open Gstaad	CL	28	€482,060
31	Jul 31	Washington, D.C.	Citi Open	H	48	$1,750,080
	Jul 31	Los Cabos	Abierto Mexicano Los Cabos	H	28	$637,395
	Jul 31	Kitzbühel	Generali Open	CL	28	€482,060
32	Aug 7	Montreal	Coupe Rogers	H	56	$4,662,300
33	Aug 13	Cincinnati	Western & Southern Open	H	56	$4,973,120
34	Aug 20	Winston-Salem	Winston-Salem Open	H	48	$664,825
35	Aug 28	New York	U.S. Open	H	128	$3,700,000
36						
37						
38	Sep 18	St. Petersburg	St. Petersburg Open	IH	28	$1,000,000
	Sep 18	Metz	Moselle Open	IH	28	€482,060
39	Sep 25	Chengdu	Chengdu Open	H	28	$1,028,885
	Sep 25	Shenzhen	Shenzhen Open	H	28	$666,960
40	Oct 2	Beijing	China Open	H	32	$3,028,080
	Oct 2	Tokyo	Rakuten Japan Open Tennis Championships	H	32	$1,563,795
41	Oct 8	Shanghai	Shanghai Rolex Masters	H	56	$5,924,890
42	Oct 16	Moscow	VTB Kremlin Cup	IH	28	$745,940
	Oct 16	Antwerp	European Open	IH	28	€589,185
	Oct 16	Stockholm	If Stockholm Open	IH	28	€589,185
43	Oct 23	Basel	Swiss Indoors Basel	IH	32	€1,837,425
	Oct 23	Vienna	Erste Bank Open 500	IH	32	€2,035,415
44	Oct 30	Paris	Rolex Paris Masters	IH	48	€4,273,775
45	Nov 7	Milan	Next Gen ATP Finals	IH	8	$1,275,000
46	Nov 17	London	ATP World Tour Finals	IH	8	$8,000,000
47						

Adapted from www.atpworldtour.com

PART ONE Winter

JANUARY 1, 2017: BRISBANE 1.0

Break point. Match point. Brisbane.

The first tournament of the year. The first day of the first month of 2017.

I had been waiting for this moment since last summer—my summer, in June; not this January Australian summer—back when my Achilles tendon tore in two and I was confined to life on a couch. I watched every single match of Wimbledon in 2016 prone and mostly alone, my family already in Barcelona when I broke myself. I was stranded but for the kindness of my neighbors and occasional visits from a few family members and friends. Unable to do much of anything else but tread through the day in a soupy haze of painkillers, I watched tennis all day, every day, to pass the time away. Singles, doubles, and then replays of the day's singles and doubles, with nowhere to be and nowhere to go, drifting in and out of sleep. As the weeks went by, I discovered that I had changed in some way that I couldn't quite describe. Following the ups and downs of players as

RANKING	MOVE	PLAYER	AGE	POINTS	TOURN PLAYED	POINTS DROPPING
1	–	Andy Murray	29	12,410	16	0
2	–	Novak Djokovic	29	11,780	17	0
3	–	Milos Raonic	25	5,450	19	0
4	–	Stan Wawrinka	31	5,315	21	0
5	–	Kei Nishikori	26	4,905	20	0
6	–	Marin Čilić	28	3,650	22	0
7	–	Gaël Monfils	30	3,625	18	0
8	–	Dominic Thiem	23	3,415	28	0
9	–	Rafael Nadal	30	3,300	16	0
10	–	Tomáš Berdych	31	3,060	21	0
11	–	David Goffin	26	2,750	24	0
12	–	Jo-Wilfried Tsonga	31	2,550	17	0
13	–	Nick Kyrgios	21	2,460	20	0
14	–	Roberto Bautista Agut	28	2,350	25	0
15	–	Lucas Pouille	22	2,156	24	0
16	–	Roger Federer	35	2,130	15	0
17	–	Grigor Dimitrov	25	2,035	25	0
18	–	Richard Gasquet	30	1,885	20	0
19	–	John Isner	31	1,850	21	0
20	–	Ivo Karlović	37	1,797	24	0

Official ATP rankings, December 26, 2016. (www.atpworldtour.com)

they followed the sun from tournament to tournament, seeing them find their groove and lose it, sometimes from one venue to the next, sometimes from one match to the next, sometimes in the middle of a point, to watch someone lose something that no one among the thousands or millions watching could see but all can feel, as though the gravity's been turned off around that player and that player alone. To watch her float into a negative zone, pulled by a phantom thread into a black cloud bank of bad results. Or, sometimes, the welcome reverse: a golden period where everything feels right, everything falls inside the court, once-impossible angles suddenly simple and seen, a reserved pocket of power found, that moment when the game becomes less about backswings and string tensions and follow-throughs and almost entirely about the feet, and eyes, they see everything early and take you there effortlessly; that moment when even the net seems on your side and bows ever so slightly as the ball you send its way passes over its thin white line. This book, in its essence, is about the things we can never quite describe but should try to because they're fleeting. I couldn't describe the tennis I was watching despite having all the time in the world to do so and oh so wanting to make sense of seeing Federer fall, a beatable Serena, Nadal all but vanish into thin air, a mojo-less Djokovic fall down a rabbit hole, and Murray finally make it to the top of the mountain. I made myself the promise that someday I would. Someday, when I could walk again and my mind wasn't saddled with sedatives, I would focus on a year and, like the players, follow the sun from beginning to end.

I'm going to go out on a limb and guess that the 2017 that happened was not the 2017 you expected. You and me both. Who could have imagined that we'd end up there? It was some strange admixture of the past and a future we weren't quite prepared for. And that this holds true for the world apart from tennis and for tennis itself is part of the power and the glory and the problem of both. As my head cleared and my body healed, I found both worlds to be, as Wallace Stevens once put it, more truly and more strange.

Break point. Match point. Brisbane.

The first tournament of the year. The first day of the first month of 2017.

I want to open the moment like a gift. The heat of January, relentless summer, the steamy gauze of the midday haze. This is the only show in town. Despite the open-air roof overhead, the heat has made everything much more difficult. Both men look like they have just emerged from a river they had accidentally fallen into. Deciding set, down 2–5, the goal now is simply to survive. To see one more point and take it from there. Bounce, bounce, think but don't think—play the percentages: find the backhand. But the serve wants to do its job too well, or the legs and mind are too tired at this point to inject any risk, and so it sets off on its launch path obedient to direction but rolling off the racket too politely. It spins safely over the net and into the service box, where the ball lands softly and, before bouncing back into the air, pauses for so long on the sweltering court that you could walk onto the court and slowly sign your name on the worn yellow felt. You were here. Finally, the ball rises and arrives to the waiting backhand return, which is dispatched back hastily and inquisitively, tit for tat to the backhand of his opponent, Elias Ymer. Let's see how he likes it. A serve to the backhand? A return to the backhand. A test? An answer. A call and a response. But they knew that the jig was up. That final serve had told them so. And so, in search of a lifeline in the form of Jordan Thompson's backhand, Ymer instead watches his own backhand sink him. His shot clips the net and doesn't even feign possibly going in. It drops as though it's run into a wall, tumbling to the court, and falls down through the o in WORLD of ATP WORLD TOUR painted across the net. The crowd cheers. Game. Set. Match. Thompson, 6–3, 6–3. In ninety minutes. The world goes on. Tennis goes on. There will be more of both. But not how anyone would have expected. It's day one of 2017. And here I am, as it happens. Still in the final, lagging American hours of 2016, hurtling toward the future as the circuit begins.

BRISBANE 2.0

The top four seeds at Brisbane were, in order, Milos Raonic, Stan Wawrinka, Kei Nishikori, and Dominic Thiem. By the end of the season, only one player on that list would even be active. But for now, in the first week of the new season, they enjoy their automatic byes into the next round, one of the more perfunctory perks of having a high ranking in smaller tournaments.

The fifth seed, in this respect, was out of luck. He would have to pick up his racket and play that extra early-round match along with the wild cards, qualifiers, and others. It was none other than Rafa Nadal. He hadn't played since October 2016, when he was upset in an early round in Shanghai by Viktor Troicki, after which he announced he was taking time off to let his sore wrist recover. Going into this new season, uncertainty swirled around Nadal. He had turned thirty in June of last season and his results indicated he was in decline, as did his increasingly creaky body. Now the iconic long hair of his heyday had been replaced by a sensible, almost businesslike cut. He was less Samson now and more Mr. Samson. Brisbane was the first step into whatever new world this was, in which there were four top players at a venue and he wasn't among them. This despite the fact that neither Djokovic nor Murray nor Federer were here. Nadal himself usually sidestepped Brisbane as well. What was he doing here? Since 2009, he had spent every year starting things up in Doha. He won there in 2014 and had been a finalist just last year in 2016. Doha was a fixture on his calendar: he even won the doubles title there a record four times. The 2017 prize money at Brisbane was $461,333; the 2017 prize money at Doha was $776,000. Perhaps Brisbane was to be the freshest of fresh starts for him. What would it have meant to him, superstitious like few others, to start this new uncertain journey in opulent Doha, where the last time he walked onto the hard court there he lost to Novak Djokovic in a nightmare of a match for him, 6–1, 6–2, and then proceeded to get knocked out in the first round of the Australian Open in heartbreaking fashion against his fellow countryman Fernando Verdasco? If 2017 was going to be a reset and a renewal, then the man who abhors change had to change. Some of the past had to be burned away. Roger was in Perth at the Hopman Cup. Let Novak and Andy slug it out in Doha. Rafa would have Brisbane with the also-rans and Stan.

He stepped out into the evening to warm applause dressed in a vivid burst of tangerine-and-white shorts. It was almost 10:30 at night. Unlike the worn-down and tenuous figure he cut throughout most of 2016, he seemed vigorous, deep in thought, dangerous to touch. He went through all of his routines. The ones he begins in the locker room with a last-second cold shower and close-quarter calisthenics, a few violent leaps straight into the air just before exiting the tunnel that leads to the court, his bag placed in its chair just so, the ID tag of his bag placed just so, his towels placed down just so, a few sips of refreshment just so, the bottles placed on the floor in front of his chair just so, just the way he likes it, no, just as it has to be, there is no other way, there's only just so. He begins to feint a sprint or two, following his routine to millimetric precision until he has to acknowledge the chair umpire and the player on the other side of the net. Then he returns to the match already being played in his mind as he warms up, his massive arms and thighs leading his thick trunk back through the epic pattern of preparation that used to strike fear in other players. But now? One wonders. He hadn't won much of anything off of clay in some time. And a younger generation of players were emerging who grew up playing with and against the type of extreme topspin Nadal had patented with his thick-framed, ultra-light Babolat racket and poly strings. Had what made him so difficult to play now also become routine? Still, there was something singular about Nadal. A lesser physical specimen would look like a walking Creamsicle in what he was wearing, but he had somehow managed to spend a lifetime making outfits no one should be able to look serious in seem full of intent. He strutted around center court like a starburst.

As much as Rafa feeds off routine, his first-round opponent, Ukraine's Alexandr Dolgopolov, feeds off its absence. Neither quite old nor young now, he has for years been a connoisseur's delight on the tour. His game is like the band you think no one has heard of, the one with too many or too few people in it, your guilty pleasure. There are the players for whom the racket is a cello. For Dolgopolov, it's a bass; he is a practitioner of arts largely distant from the highest levels of the circuit; where others try to construct, he deconstructs; he is a disciple of the School of the Chaos Point. There's a technical term for it: he has funky game.

Sometimes it looks like he's given up on a point, unwilling to submit himself to the discipline of riding out the undulations and give-some-get-some nature of difficult rallies, the kind that test your patience as much as your footwork and groundstrokes—the alpha and omega of Nadal's approach. But things are so often not what they seem. Dolgopolov suffers from Gilbert's syndrome, a chronic condition that affects the liver's ability to produce bilirubin, which is the natural by-product of the hemoglobin in our red blood cells when they are broken down by the body. While it's non-lethal, it causes sudden and extreme exhaustion. Things that exacerbate it include constant travel and physical exertion: basically, being a tennis professional. When he was diagnosed with Gilbert's he was already a promising youth player. He ignored the doctor's advice to scrap any idea of playing at the level his promise suggested he was destined for. Instead, he cultivated a game over the years to correspond with his unpredictable reserves of energy. He tries to end a point as soon as the first glimpse of an opportunity presents itself: an early, unexpected drop shot from an unlikely position on the court; a low-percentage forehand down the line when a safe crosscourt shot is begging to be hit; a backhand slice seeking out an ambitious, eye-popping angle. When it works, it's oohs and ahhs and cheers from the gallery. When it doesn't, crickets. Sometimes it's champagne stuff from him. Other times, when the muse has abandoned him, a Dolgopolov performance can be tough to swallow. Don't let the big swings and bellowing grunts fool you: tennis is a sport of deception and surprise. The more disguise you can manage into your groundstrokes and your serve, the more chances you have of robbing your opponent of that vital fraction of a second. In the bigger picture, tennis remains the same.

He's been ranked as high as thirteenth in the world on the back of a scintillating 2011 when he appeared to announce himself as the next great talent in tennis at age twenty-two. He entered Brisbane and the start of 2017 mired in a cloud of bad results and ranked sixty-second in the world, descending to a level he hadn't seen his name near in close to seven years. He warms up a little more languidly than Nadal. Everyone does. The racket in his hand is clearly a Wilson Pro Staff, but it's missing the familiar w stenciled on the strings. Bad results have left him a free agent: a player without a racket sponsor. Later in the year, a gambling watchdog unit will wonder about some of the statistical outliers in his matches (going a whole match without seeing a break point, for instance) and the even stranger betting lines that followed him around from tournament to tournament. His results will pick up on the heels of it as though he were chased into good form: a final in Båstad, Sweden, at the Swedish Open in July; a good run to the round of sixteen at the U.S. Open in August; a final in Shenzhen, China, at the Shenzhen Open in October; he'll end the year ranked thirty-eighth. The child of a professional coach, he started playing the game at three years old, coached then as he is now by his father: you've heard the story before, you'll hear it again.

He is in his late twenties, just under six feet tall, with an angular face and soft expressionless eyes that contradict his hollow cheeks. He sports a ponytail and a hair band to keep his hair out of his eyes. No goatee tonight, he is relatively clean-shaven, wearing a white crew top with thin sky-blue lines across the front, a thick sky-blue racing stripe along the sides and sleeves, and matching solid sky-blue sneakers and shorts. Tonight, he can't get a first serve in and Nadal feasts on his compromised second serve, dispatching him in straight sets: 6–3, 6–3. True to his playing style, Dolgopolov started as fast as he possibly could. He broke Nadal's serve early and had tallied eleven winners by the time Rafa registered his first. But Dolgopolov cooled off as quickly as he had started hot. The unforced errors swiftly began to pile up. Shots that at the start were dropping inside the court began to betray his racket. He finished the match with fifty-six errors, thirty-two of them unforced. At one point during the match, Dolgopolov, angry with the world, stormed off the court and returned having changed his shorts. It didn't help. He was twisted up, his funky game flat. How much was it him, and how much was it the man on the other side of the net? For, while Nadal had never been a player to rack up a huge number of winners, his anemic numbers were, despite the final score, startling—a mere six winners total: two aces, two from the backhand side, one smash, one volley, and not a single one from the forehand. Yet, his serve showed more promise than it had in some time. It was almost as though he had inverted his strengths. Only time would tell.

Regardless, you wouldn't say that it was vintage Nadal, for how he played or for the context. Now he was like the other twenty-four players obliged to play in the first round of this relatively small tournament—there were thirty-two spaces in comparison to the 128 for the majors (i.e., the Grand Slams), 250 points instead of the 2,000 at stake in the majors, 1,000 in the Masters. The top four got a day or two off as a gift for showing up. But the others were the players who had to grind from day one. We know now that Nadal hasn't yet fallen into that category, but as Brisbane 2017 began, the world wondered what to make of the Bull in winter. And we were left without a clear answer, as two nights later Milos Raonic took a punch from Nadal before answering back by winning two straight sets with all the robust confidence one would expect from the higher-ranked player: 4–6, 6–3, 6–4. Murray and Djokovic, the number one and two, we'd grown accustomed, slowly, to seeing have Nadal's number. But now Milos Raonic? The Clark Graebner we didn't ask for but deserve? Is this where Nadal is now? Where are we?

Step back from the ocean-blue Plexicushion hard courts of the Queensland Tennis Centre, and you'll discover yourself to be not in Brisbane but rather in Tennyson, a tiny suburb named after the English Victorian poet Alfred, Lord Tennyson—"Lawn Tennyson," the "gentleman poet," as Stephen Dedalus refers to him in *Ulysses*. Step even further back—from Australia on New Year's Day, cross the Pacific, climb to the equator—and you will find yourself not in the summer of Down Under but in the northern hemisphere's winter.

Playing before a home crowd, Thompson fights his way to the third round by beating perennial overachiever and former world number four David Ferrer of Spain before meeting his baker in Japan's Kei Nishikori, who whipped him up a breadstick for each set, 6–1, 6–1 (a breadstick is one game won in a set, a bagel is zero games won: they are signs of dishonor). Ranked fifth in the world at the start of 2017 and a consolidated top-ten player for a couple of years, Nishikori was set for a run at the things he had yet to accomplish on the circuit: a ranking in the top three (he'd been as high as fourth) and a title in a major (he was a finalist in the 2014 U.S. Open). The 2016 U.S. Open was almost as kind to him: he lost in the semifinals after defeating Andy Murray in the quarterfinals. It would prove to be the last time Murray would lose a match in 2016. Short in stature and lightning-quick, gifted with a two-handed backhand that could absorb and redirect his opponent's pace on the short hop, but somewhat held back—from the very highest heights of the game—by his capable but unreliable forehand, serve, and fitness, Nishikori was a smaller prototype of the mold that made Murray and Novak Djokovic, the top two players on the circuit. He had turned twenty-seven on the twenty-ninth of December. In the new logic of tennis, where teenagers fight for scraps on the lower Challenger circuit, he was entering his prime. In the semifinal of Brisbane he squared off against the player who beat him in the 2016 U.S. Open semifinal, Stan Wawrinka, who went on to win the tournament and notch his third major title in three years. Nishikori would get a measure of revenge on Wawrinka in November of that year by beating him in sixty-seven minutes in London at the ATP World Tour Finals. These types of minimum-resistance capitulations on non–Grand Slam stages had become par for the course for Wawrinka, who, by this time in his early thirties, had become a player who reserved his considerable gifts for the major tournaments and, as a rule, offered far less resistance anywhere else. At Brisbane, after losing the first set in a tiebreaker, Nishikori wins the final two sets by a whisker. Wawrinka pretends to be bothered, but his mind is really on Melbourne and the Australian Open. What's important at this point for Nishikori, however, is the scoreline. He needs results; they're proof that he can handle the few players on the circuit ahead of him and, rather crucially, that his body can handle the pounding of going deep into tournaments and not betray him as it did in

2016 in Wimbledon when he had to forfeit mid-match due to injury, and not for the first time. What to do when your Achilles' heel is your body, all of it?

On the other side of the Brisbane draw was the number one seed: the Canadian Milos Raonic. He started the year with a career-high ranking of third in the world and had won Brisbane the year before, defeating Federer in the 2016 final. Later in that same year, Raonic played a key role at Wimbledon when in the semifinal he defeated Federer once again, half by the blunt force of his game and half by being smart enough not to get in the way of a clearly hobbled Roger getting in the way of himself. Raonic's game is one part serve and one part ambition. The other parts are still works in progress, but he speaks with such certainty that sometimes it seems even he forgets that they are. "I am by no means done," he told the press in the media room after his victory over Federer on Wimbledon's famed Centre Court. He was done, though. Two days later, he delivered one of the more tepid performances of a Wimbledon finalist that you'll ever see. Facing the local favorite, Murray, and finally in position to fulfill his promise, he wilted. But, like Nishikori, he regained steam at the World Tour Finals, where this time he pushed Murray, who was again playing before a home crowd, to the brink.

Despite not winning a single tournament in 2016, he spoke of himself as a top player on the tour, and the ranking of third going into 2017 seemed to satisfy his sense of himself and his tennis. On the third day in Brisbane, he faced the ninth-ranked Rafa Nadal.

If Raonic was ascendant, what, then, was Grigor Dimitrov? A player graced with such precocious, easy-on-the-eye gifts that he was given the nickname Baby Fed, he nevertheless showed up at Brisbane already a bit of an afterthought on the men's circuit. Having reached the top ten in the summer of 2014, he almost immediately thereafter went on a mysterious descent of form that ended with him falling to fortieth in the rankings by July 2016. Of the three great promises in their mid-twenties, Dimitrov, unlike Raonic and Nishikori, didn't hold form at the very-good-but level; he sank. Quietly, however, the late summer and a new coach brought better results. By Brisbane he was ranked seventeenth. He was talked about less than his peers, all of whom he had peaked ahead of. He'd had his time; now was theirs. Dimitrov's first big challenge of 2017 was to reestablish a pecking order that had him somewhere, anywhere, in it. On the third day of Brisbane, he beat the player talked about now as he once was: the twenty-three-year-old Austrian Dominic Thiem, ranked eighth in the world and the fourth seed of the tournament. Then he turned Raonic over in the semifinal, winning the first-set tiebreak 9–7 and then running away with the second set 6–2. The next day, he beat Nishikori in three sets. The first champion of the 2017 season was Grigor Dimitrov of Bulgaria. He's widely considered one of the nicest guys on the circuit. Blessed with balletic movement and easy power, Dimitrov is the prototype of the stylish player. He has a long, powerful forehand and sweeping one-handed backhand. The strong traces of a tennis era gone by that you see in Roger Federer's game are the residue of the tennis he loved as a kid. And the strong traces of Roger Federer's game in Grigor Dimitrov's game are the residue of his love of Roger as a kid. As Grigor was breaking through the top ranks of the main circuit, the similarities between the two players were so unmistakable that thanks to them Dimitrov ended up carrying a burden no young player should have: he was given that blessed curse of a nickname, Baby Fed. His results in recent years were such that the nickname's days were numbered. He was no longer a baby and he wasn't any closer to winning Grand Slams. But if the end of 2016 was promising, beginning 2017 with a title was the chance to consolidate his potential from week one of the new year. Like Nishikori and Raonic, Dimitrov wasn't among the youngest generation on the circuit. But his story was still there to be written with his racket if he was up for it.

Was he Baby Fed again? Or had he evolved? Was he in sync with his past, or had he broken free headlong toward the future? Whatever it was to be, Brisbane was now part of the answer.

DOHA

"This is what we wanted!" the commentator Simon Reed intoned into his microphone at the end of the fourteen-shot rally, his voice almost sounding bored with the statement, so crisp and certain it was. "The best two players on the planet really laying into each other!"

It's the seventh day of 2017: a Saturday in January in Doha, Qatar. A short walk from the commercial buildings, shops, and restaurants adorning Doha's city center is the Khalifa International Tennis and Squash Complex, home of the Qatar ExxonMobil Open since the year of its founding in 1993. Over these twenty-five years, this 250 tournament has become a destination stop for the game's best players. Brisbane may offer players the chance to get acclimated to Australia in preparation for the Australian Open, but Doha offers a different type of spectacle and luxury of a different degree. By summer of 2017, nine sovereign governments will have severed diplomatic ties with Qatar, including to go as far as to withdraw ambassadors and institute trade and travel bans. At this early part of the year, the White House is about to change hands. Both domestic and foreign policy for the future are completely up in the air. Brexit is or isn't but definitely is happening. In France, the upcoming presidential race is under way and—like in the United States and in the United Kingdom—the fate of the very idea of what France is seems to be on the ticket. The world feels slippery, dense, supercharged with social and political change—and yet for a few hours here was tennis, literally a light in the sleepy darkness of my apartment. It's moments like this, these odd hours with the game on, when its metronome and angles take the form of therapy—I listen to the world take a deep breath. Suddenly, in thinking about Doha again, it all feels so present. Not just the matches, but what they were supposed to mean. Qatar was supposed to be the herald of a new era. Qatar was supposed to change the world.

This was the circuit's big heavyweight bout, round one of who knows how many during the year. This was the new normal going forward. After a decade of four tennis legends battling it out year after year for supremacy in their sport, enhancing each other, elevating each other's standards and shifting positions in the hierarchy at the absolute summit of the circuit, now only two legends were left standing. And here they were. This was how the year was destined to really get started. This wasn't to be missed.

This is what we wanted.

The two best players on the planet really laying into each other.

The 2017 final of the Qatar Open. Don't forget it. And when you remember it, speak of it as what it was: a song of the new year to the melody of the year that had just passed—2017 in the key of 2016, back when we thought we were getting what we wanted, the two best players on the planet really laying into each other, back when there was Andy Murray and Novak Djokovic . . . and then there was everyone else.

Before we sing a song of Federer and Nadal, before Murray and Djokovic disappear, reappear, and then disappear again, remember that there was Doha 2017. It was supposed to be the big bang but ended up being the whimper.

It was supposed to be the story of 2017. How Murray finally, after so many torturous years of crying, growling, recriminating his team, and eviscerating himself, had risen to the number one ranking, and how then he would fare in defending it. And how the unconquerable Djokovic, now having finally won all four Grand Slam titles, would react to suddenly and rather unexpectedly being saddled with the number two ranking. No one was on the horizon to challenge them; they played three-hour, five-hour matches with hardly the need to sit. Insanely fit, flexible, and fundamentally defensive players by nature, they had become impossible to pass either on the court or in the rankings (except for occasional guest appearances on the circuit of Stan Wawrinka at his peak). Murray, who wears the underdog role like cashmere, found himself in the unprecedented position of top dog. And Djokovic, unplayable as recently as just last June, was inexplicably somehow now in the role of the chaser.

Three weeks from today, Rod Laver Arena in Melbourne will be the stage for another Roger and Rafa. We'll call them the best two players on the planet again and then again, although we won't mean it. Not then, not yet. Then, the vintage feel in the throat when you say it will give way to a simple, dull act of veracity you recognize from before. The Swiss and the Spaniard will have settled back into their perches in the rankings by then. But for now we're here in Qatar. It's the seventh day of 2017, a Saturday in January in Doha. It's a moment that sits like a stunned and stunted rock in the midst of a surging stream. A classic that was to define the year. Was this not what we wanted? Great tennis, fun tennis, something to inject a little joy into the world's grimness. A classic that ended up having absolutely nothing to do with reality. There they were: the two best players on the planet not named Roger or Rafael or Serena. Slowly, we all had come to grips with this. We became fluent in it. This was what we wanted. The two best players on the planet really laying into each other. You say it until you mean it. But then you meant it and it was gone.

When Murray and Djokovic play, you can see the match almost as well with your eyes closed and your ears open, listening for their footwork, the skidding, the relentless scuffing of their shoes on the court, an occasionally desperate grunt to coax out that vital extra half step, and then a short stoppage of play and a patch of silence before they do it again. Together they were heralds of tennis's new form of dominance: sadistic resilience and rugged precision, with shot patterns dangerous enough to threaten but safe enough to guarantee that they'd stay in.

Murray had been great at it for close to a decade.

Born in 1987, he grew up in the town of Dunblane in the center of Scotland. He attended Dunblane Primary School, where he and his older brother, Jamie, were when in March 1996 an armed man carrying registered guns entered the school and murdered sixteen children and one teacher before killing himself. One of the worst mass shootings in the history of Britain, it led to two Firearms Acts being passed in 1997. Murray's parents split when he was ten, and he learned tennis from his mother, Judy, who was a coach. For the sake of his development he eventually moved to Barcelona for a year and a half to live and train at the Sánchez-Casal Academy under the tutelage of Emilio Sánchez, a three-time Grand Slam champion in doubles. Murray's route to tennis stardom was measured but hardly slow. He was an elite junior player, turned pro in 2005, won his first title, and, upon attaining the ranking of forty-two in February 2006, became Britain's top-ranked player. In 2007 he became a top-ten player, and in 2008 he played his first Grand Slam final, losing to Federer in straight sets at the U.S. Open. By this point he had become a fixture at the deepest stages of tournaments: a top-five player capable of winning some of the bigger 250s—Doha, Marseille, St. Petersburg—but he still stood on the other side of the chasm from Roger and Rafa, a chasm that Djokovic was already in the process of crossing.

Between 2009 and 2011, he upped his title haul, becoming a regular title-contender at the prestigious Masters 1000s. He also took on a new coach, letting Àlex Corretja go in favor of Ivan Lendl, who convinced Murray to add a bit more initiative into his play to complement his world-class powers of reaction and adaptation. Lendl's stoic, no-nonsense demeanor became a stay against Murray's constant complaining, moaning, and recriminating of the box of seats where his coaches, family, and associates sat. Also, Lendl's having won eight Grand Slam titles himself and holding on to the number one ranking for an astonishing 270 weeks during the eighties, when Connors, McEnroe, Edberg, Mats Wilander, and Boris Becker were all in their prime, added some gravitas to his instruction of a player in Murray who was now winning everything there was to win—aside from the biggest titles of them all, the Grand Slams. And here was where Lendl could help Murray profoundly by way of having lost eleven Grand Slam finals to go along with the eight he won. Murray needed to learn not only how to win Grand Slam finals, he also needed to learn what to do with all of the losses.

He rarely had that little extra to overcome Federer, Nadal, or Djokovic. Entering Doha in 2017, his record against the three of them stood at twenty-nine wins and fifty-five losses. Of the forty-seven Grand Slam titles won by the Big Four, Murray had won three—Stan Wawrinka and his big, risk-embracing power game owned just as many and at three different Grand Slams (although Murray easily lapped him in the overall trophy count).

And yet, Murray's success was singular: his Olympic gold medals and Wimbledon titles granted him a type of Anglo gravitas akin to a writer's writer or a band that only recorded a few albums, all of them classics. The doubter would say he'd lost eight Grand Slam finals. The supporter would say he'd played in eleven Grand Slam finals. Similar to his game, what he was in the grand scheme of things always limned an edge. He'd amassed legendary, unprecedented success. But as late as the fall of 2016 it looked like he would never attain the rudimentary mark of a great player: the number one ranking.

Murray was rock-solid in his position as the second-ranked player in the world. Federer and Nadal were injured and inconsistency crept up on them with age. Meanwhile, Djokovic casually kept Murray at arm's length from the top spot. More than with any other player, Murray's career was playing out exactly as he played: he chased, he endured, and he was good enough to beat everybody else.

But the fall of 2016 changed Murray's fortunes. Djokovic failed to defend his Wimbledon title, falling to Sam Querrey over three days and looking haggard and absent in doing so. This was the start of a spiral that affected his form first—Djokovic would win his next tournament, the prestigious Masters 1000 in Toronto in early August 2016, but looked like a shell of himself doing so; his opponents seemed in disbelief that a player who had been practically unbeatable for the past two years could appear now so flat: they fell over themselves to lose to him, as though that's what they should do . . . Djokovic, meanwhile, would tend to his left arm between points and look up to his support team in the stands with a glare of bemusement one moment and a blank stare of befuddlement the next. Something was not right. But such was Djokovic's greatness, the height at which he was playing, that even a dip in form left him with enough to make a final. The luck of the draw helped him reach the U.S. Open final. He started fast in the first set and held on, barely, to win that one. Then he found himself on the receiving end of Wawrinka's onslaught. He took time off after, and reappeared for the end-of-the-year tournament in London. And once again, he seemed blunted but was good enough to reach the final. By this point, Murray had won every tournament he entered between New York and London. While Djokovic took time to figure himself out, Murray won—in order—the 500-point tournament in Beijing, the 1,000-point tournament in Shanghai, the 500-point tournament in Vienna, and the 1,000-point tournament in Paris, and then beat Djokovic in the final tournament of 2016, the 1,500-point ATP World Tour Finals, which left him rather unbelievably with the prestigious year-end top ranking for the first time in his career. It was a chase-down, snatch-and-grab act of epic proportions to end the year. As Murray rose to number one, the curtain closed on the year. Doha 2017 was to become both the start of a new chapter and a postscript to the last.

And it was. Until it wasn't.

In retrospect, the cracks in the disastrous year that both Murray and Djokovic would end up having were there for all to see in Doha. In the first set of the first round, Murray, facing Jérémy Chardy of France, raced out to a 6–0 lead. Andy won the next set in a tiebreaker (7–2). In his second-round match he won the first set against Gerald Melzer in a tiebreaker (8–6) and the second set 7–5—total time: two hours and twenty-three minutes. In the quarterfinals Murray won the first set against Spain's Nicolás Almagro in a tiebreaker (7–4) and then won the second set 7–5—total time: two hours and ten minutes. And then seemed to right himself against his first seeded opponent, perennial top-ten player Tomáš Berdych, whom he beat 6–3, 6–4, but he took another hour and forty-one minutes to do it. The final against Djokovic would take two hours and fifty-four minutes. Murray was spending an obscene amount of time on the court. It's one thing to be locked in three tight sets in a match against Djokovic. It's another entirely to be consistently locked into long battles against the rest of the field. Murray wasn't making quick work of anyone: he simply couldn't get off the court.

But the results were with him.

Later in 2017, at Wimbledon, Murray would hobble through the end of a defeat to Sam Querrey, the same player who had taken down Djokovic at the same tournament the prior year. His hip would fail him, as had his shoulder earlier in the year. Dogged physicality, living every point to its last possible end, being a wall: these were the building blocks by which Andy Murray rose to the heights of the game in an era when he could have been content with being a heroic loser, a rich man's also-ran, and no one would have begrudged him it. At least not any more than they do now, for he simply isn't as seductive as Federer or Nadal, or as successful as Djokovic, or as romantic as Wawrinka. We saw him battle through to the final at Doha and thought, *Andy Murray knows how to win*. And he did now. And how! With his win against Berdych he was on a twenty-eight-match win streak. The results were the results. But the results were coming from having to rev his engine further to its limits than he should.

Meanwhile, on the other side of the draw, Djokovic was crushing through the early rounds. He handled the sixty-third-ranked Jan-Lennard Struff, seventy-first-ranked Horacio Zeballos, and one-hundred-and-seventh-ranked Radek Štěpánek with ease. Then in the semifinal he found himself in a deep hole against the veteran Madrid-born Fernando Verdasco, ranked forty-second at the time and on good days a handful for anyone, even at thirty-three years of age. Djokovic, for his part, was looking as gaunt as he ever had, not slender or slim but approaching skeletal, as though his body were feeding on itself from bottom to top, culminating in a sucked-out space on each side of his face where his cheeks used to be flush with life, and two dark vacancies where his eyes should be. This was compounded by his body language, an amalgam of fidgeting and wry slumps of the shoulders regardless of whether things went for or against him. At times, between points, he looked up in the crowd to the box where his coach and trainer were seated and offered them a blank stare that softened into a smirk, as though they were strangers who'd won a contest to sit in those seats and he had little interest in who they were or why they were there.

Despite all this, he is an all-time talent, hardwired with the instinctive aspects of his game—one is his unparalleled return of serve, another his easy absorption and redirection of pace on both forehand and backhand—that make him extremely difficult to beat. He uses these to race out to a 4–2 lead to start the match. Then, suddenly, he becomes a shell of himself and vanishes. He doesn't win another game in the frame, and, even worse, gets broken at love twice in a row. Verdasco wins the first set 6–4.

The second set knots at the end: 6–6. They go to a tiebreaker. Win it, and Verdasco is on to an unexpected final against Murray. Lose it, and he lives to fight on for another set, but he'll also have given life to the most lethal closer of the past half decade. Yes, Djokovic has been that good for that long. Verdasco played his way to a 6–2 lead. He only needed to win one more point out of the next four to win the match. Worse still for Djokovic, on this first match point he's the one serving and his serve hasn't been kind to him this night. At moments like these, on serve with everything to play for, Djokovic is known to bend forward at the baseline and bounce the ball relentlessly before starting the point. Most players bounce the ball a handful of times before going into their service motion, something in the range of four bounces or so. When nervous Djokovic routinely bounces the ball over twenty times before a serve, I imagine him rewinding in his mind how he got from finally winning the French Open in 2016 and completing the career Grand Slam and a continent-wide lead in the ATP Tour rankings to the spot where he is now, a semifinal in Doha, down four match points to Fernando Verdasco, carrying the bad mojo of the end of last season when he lost at Wimbledon, the U.S. Open, and the ATP Tour Final, and, for the first time since the summer of 2014 was ranked something other than first in the world. Bounce bounce bounce bounce bouncebouncebouncebouncebouncebouncebouncebounce . . .

Somewhere between Djokovic canceling all four of Verdasco's match points with clutch play and Verdasco gift-wrapping them with nervous play lies the truth of tennis. One step in the wrong direction in the middle of one point can cause an avalanche that sweeps away any advantage, no matter its size. Opportunity's door opens and closes quickly, quicker than in most other sports. Verdasco tightens, reads his lines, plays the role of Fernando Verdasco. On the longer exchanges he hesitates before stepping forward, then retreats back; on the shorter ones, he sprays mishit forehands into the stands. A few people in the crowd, disappointed with his drop in play, begin to hiss.

Djokovic uses his two-handed backhand to take control of the early points. He has an undeterred ability to hit dangerous balls to all parts of the court with sufficient margin that they're safely inside the lines. He doesn't paint lines, he shadows them. The skill to hit these types of groundstrokes error-free and consistently gives his opponent little room for air or time to think.

Djokovic had finally rediscovered this core aspect of his game: he had reset. Verdasco was suddenly caught in a web of indecision. Should he continue to attack? He tried to take the initiative, serving for the match 6–3 in the tiebreaker, and shanked a ball into the stands. Or should he wait for Djokovic to make an error? The next point they played was a twenty-nine-shot rally that eventually ended with Verdasco blinking and hitting out. No one does the Safety Dance like Djokovic. Murray is close, but Djokovic has a strange ability to twist through the vise he seems trapped in and somehow squeeze the life out of his opponent instead. It's not a pretty magic, but it's magic all the same.

THE DOHA FINAL

Despite Murray taking the longest path possible to get there and despite Djokovic being dragged to the brink by Verdasco, there had been an air of inevitability that the number one and number two would meet in the final. And that air of inevitability about the number one and number two meeting in the final papered over most concerns about their form. Both of them had long ago mastered the art of manageable suffering. Djokovic did it more like a passive-aggressive dance, a loose-limbed tango; Murray, a game of cat-and-mouse.

The start of the seventh game of the first set of the first big final of the year. It was only a 250 tournament, as small as they get on the elite circuit, but it was to be the first statement match of 2017, the first clarion call of the new order of things finally cut free from the annoyance of the past. Finally, it was just Murray and Djokovic: one vs. two, slugging it out for tennis supremacy in the desert night, miles clear of all the pretenders and the two past glories on the tour.

Act one, scene one of the way things were going to be from now on.

Three-games-all in the first set of the best-of-three, first point of the seventh game. Djokovic takes a long, deep breath, bounces the ball just in front of his left foot again and again and again, and then, finally, rocks back ever so slightly and starts his serve. Murray had just navigated through his own tough hold of serve, which included a twenty-eight-shot rally at 40–40 that he survived using, as he often does, a defensive lob to steady himself in the point and then, after a few well-shaped crosscourt forehand conversations, punctuated it with a well-disguised forehand drop shot. The two started breathing heavily from the first points of the match. Djokovic is at least thankful there's no wind tonight, unlike other nights in Doha where he had to contend with a continually troublesome gale gliding in off the Persian Gulf. Both are inclined to stretch a point out until it turns sheer and they can see an opening. When they play each other it's an added exertion, their matches against each other tending to rumble on, each waiting on the other to make a mistake. Murray's been the one to blink in these encounters most of the time, although just this past November, in the last tournament of 2016 in London, Murray had beaten Djokovic to end the year as the top-ranked player for the first time in his career.

Despite his tall frame, to which over the years he's added much muscle, Murray isn't a particularly powerful player, nor is he one imbued with much in the way of grace. He wears oversized wristbands that cover most of his forearms, and a baseball cap covering his unkempt waves of hair that nevertheless still sometimes spill out from the sides; wrapped up and dour on the court, he reminds me of a beekeeper about to enter a hive. He lumbers around the court, and yet his feet are stunning in their quickness: he gets to just about everything, rarely making it look or sound easy. Indeed, there's little quiet in the way he moves. When he stretches to chase down a difficult shot sent his way from the other side of the net, an under-duress yell often precedes his legs firing into action like the loud engine of a muscle car sputtering before it revs up, rears back, and jumps into its speed. He's lightning-quick. Not just of body but also of mind. England has embraced him as their noble (and now knighted) champion, but his game reflects the streetwise Scot in him. He lives off of wry chicanery hidden in his consistency; his shot pattern screws with his opponents' rhythm, often lulling them into a false sense of expectation. Imagine being given a Russian nesting doll and opening it, working your way through one carbon copy of the same doll after another, until you come across one with an egg yolk stowed inside it that spills onto your lap. This is what it's like to play him. One of Murray's trademarks is the way he can turn a desperate reach for an opponent's would-be winner into a ridiculously high and probing lob, one that hangs in the air long enough both to get him back into proper position on the court and to ask some questions of his opponent's nerve as he waits for it to drop. Time is a tennis player's ally, except when it's not. The complications of handling a lob—the change of eye level, the broken rhythm of the court, and the supposed ease of an overhead smash in the sudden will-he-or-won't-he silence of the moment—have coaxed embarrassing errors out of all kinds of players. It's been perhaps the most glaring weakness in Djokovic's game, and from the outset of the Doha final Murray didn't hesitate when stretched by an angled Djokovic groundstroke to respond with a lob. But time and time again, Djokovic was ready for them. The two players punched and counterpunched over three tight sets. Having shaken free of the past, they played as if the future began there and then in the nascent days of January 2017, which for the first time would be all about them.

"This is what we wanted! The best two players on the planet really laying into each other."

Djokovic would win 6–3, 5–7, 6–4 after a grueling two hours and fifty-four minutes. Grueling but exhilarating—there was a lightness in their play usually absent in their matches against each other. They played as though they seemed to know that, perhaps for the first time, they were the pairing everyone was waiting to see. They had no one to worry about for the next three to four years but each other . . . and themselves.

Djokovic would take the win in stride. "To start off the year with a win over the number one in the world and the biggest rival," he said rather sanguinely after the match, "it's a dream start, so I am hoping I can get the best out of it."

Two matches later, Djokovic loses to a wild card: Denis Isto-min of Uzbekistan, the 117th-ranked player in the world. Bowing out of the Australian Open—a Grand Slam he's won twice on the trot and six times overall—in the second round, he says after the match, "There was not much I could do."

Andy Murray would fare little better, making it only through three rounds.

And just like that, what Doha was vanished. No one ever spoke of it again.

THE IDEA OF ORDER AT THE AUSTRALIAN OPEN

With Donald Trump's inauguration on the horizon, in the count-down to it there was no escaping the fact that January felt inher-ently weird. A different kind of weird, though. Not the typical I-keep-writing-last-year's-date-down kind of weird, but rather something sad and cantankerous. A restless unhappiness circulated among many of us, a haggard sagging of the soul accompanied by an unquenchable need to share it. We are more efficient than ever in sharing our unhappiness. And we have practically mastered disguising our discomfort with wry, distant cynicism. We meme as much as we mean. But sometimes we're still able to surprise our-selves and hit the streets.

January 2017 was an event horizon we all crossed kicking and screaming. There was no way out but forward, into the uncertainty of an unfamiliar world. And at the center of it was the Australian Open, which began on the sixteenth—the same day that Gaius Julius Caesar Octavianus took on the title of Augustus, the first edition of *Don Quixote* was published, Hitler moved into his under-ground bunker, and—this particular year—we observed Martin Luther King Jr. Day. We watched tennis together in the middle of

RANKING	MOVE	PLAYER	AGE	POINTS	TOURN PLAYED	POINTS DROPPING
1	_	Andy Murray	29	12,560	17	1,200
2	_	Novak Djokovic	29	11,780	17	2,000
3	_	Milos Raonic	26	5,290	19	720
4	_	Stan Wawrinka	31	5,155	21	180
5	_	Kei Nishikori	27	5,010	20	360
6	_	Gaël Monfils	30	3,625	18	360
7	_	Marin Čilić	28	3,605	22	90
8	_	Dominic Thiem	23	3,415	28	90
9	_	Rafael Nadal	30	3,195	16	10
10	_	Tomáš Berdych	31	3,060	21	360
11	_	David Goffin	26	2,750	24	180
12	_	Jo-Wilfried Tsonga	31	2,505	17	180
13	^1	Nick Kyrgios	21	2,460	20	90
14	v1	Roberto Bautista Agut	28	2,350	24	180
15	_	Grigor Dimitrov	25	2,135	24	90
16	_	Lucas Pouille	22	2,131	24	10
17	_	Roger Federer	35	1,980	14	720
18	_	Richard Gasquet	30	1,885	20	0
19	_	John Isner	31	1,850	21	180
20	^3	Jack Sock	24	1,810	19	45

Official ATP rankings, January 16, 2017. (www.atpworldtour.com)

the night, you and I. Maybe you skipped Brisbane, Doha, Chennai, Auckland, and Sydney, but I know you were up with me for Melbourne. Either you couldn't sleep or you needed something to take your mind off the day while Orwell's *1984* flew off real and virtual bookshelves. You knew the Australian Open wasn't going to either change or save the world, but you decided to take a peek anyway at any odd hour you could, because tennis

Djokovic and Murray holding the winner and runner-up trophies during the post-match celebration in Doha, January 7, 2017. (Anadolu Agency / Getty Images)

can offer what Robert Frost said poetry provides: a momentary stay against confusion.

And so it was slightly past dawn and you and I were up. The sky is a dull file-cabinet gray. A thick morning chill scours down on the thin morning light. People hurry by under umbrellas, a few loiter on corners up and down the street, bareheaded, waiting for a car or a bus, newspapers tucked under their arms. This is how the year begins. It's that time of year when winter is pulled by the end of the year on one side and on the other by the start of the year. It becomes sheer, so translucent you can almost see through it. The world feels topsy-turvy—fuzzed. We're in Australia and I am in New York.

And therefore, as the calendar year starts and a new tennis season begins, you may find your senses thrown off a little. At least I do, watching a midsummer sport in midwinter in the middle of the night. Whether I stay up through the night to watch or get up far earlier than I should, I drift and am used to drifting, and after all, it's only tennis. Isn't it? It's January, and 2017 has a vise grip on the mind. And here I am, groggy as hell, keeping up with news about tennis from sixteen hours in the future.

During this long January of discontent, I've found it especially difficult to turn away from tennis. Despite the lack of sleep, these middle-of-the-night siren songs have served me well—for the most part. Nine at night. Eleven at night. Three in the morning. While avid viewers of the World Cup or the Olympics only spend a couple of weeks every four years waking up at some godforsaken early hour to catch a glimpse of their sport of choice, tennis fans go through this every year, since the circuit starts the year in Australia. The new season clears its throat in Brisbane and then sets right off, full throttle, into the fraying world.

Tennis is a game I inherited from my parents. I'm old enough to have played with a wooden racket, but not old enough to have played seriously with a wooden racket. I'm also the age of perhaps the last generation of teenage champions. When I was a kid, seeing another kid win Wimbledon (as Boris Becker did in 1985 at the tender age of seventeen years, 227 days) or the French Open (as Michael Chang did in 1989 at the tender age of seventeen years, 110 days) was a big deal but not unfathomable; difficult but not unthinkable; far from the earth-shattering spectacle it would be today, when players in their mid-twenties are considered up-and-coming.

In retrospect, I was part of a generation of latchkey kids whose favorite tennis players were teenagers, favorite rappers were teenagers, favorite doctor was a teenager (Doogie Howser, M.D.). Tennis, in other words, fit seamlessly into my vision of the world as being low-hanging fruit for youth. And while Monica Seles lost some prime seasons because of having been literally stabbed in the back, and Michael Chang never again won a major after winning one at seventeen; while Steffi Graf retired at twenty-nine because she'd already done everything she wanted, and Boris Becker played in a style that eventually drained every ounce of champion vigor his younger self had brimmed with; while Jennifer Capriati—a pro at thirteen and a French Open semifinalist at fifteen—learned to love the game after losing her way, what didn't change was the ode to youth that tennis proved to be. When you're in your teens, words like *resilience*, *endurance*, and *perspective* aren't real.

At the turn of the millennium, when I'd become invested in those words, I began to look at tennis differently. Becker was gone by then and Chang was no longer a top player, but Seles and Capriati were back and almost as good as ever. And the very back end of the last great teen generation—Venus Williams, Serena Williams, Roger Federer, and a little later Rafa Nadal—well, they were doing okay.

Going forth into adulthood, this had given me heart and

perspective. I saw players I knew from my youth, or thought I knew in the way that young people think they know distant stars, grow and change; they matured. Andre Agassi first introduced the great late version of himself as a player to the world at the Australian Open when he won it in 2000, then again in 2001 and 2003. It was the last Grand Slam Monica Seles won before being stabbed in the back by a deranged Steffi Graf fan as she rested in her chair during a changeover, and the only Grand Slam she would win after her comeback. It's where Serena Williams made her Grand Slam debut, in 1998 at the age of sixteen, and, in the same year, where she and Venus would play their first professional match against each other in the second round. And since 2004, Rod Laver Arena has been the virtual exclusive playground of the Big Four among the men: only twice has someone not named Federer, Djokovic, Nadal, or Murray won since then—Marat Safin in 2005 and Wawrinka in 2014. The Australian Open has long been like an idea of order: arranging, deepening, enchanting from the other side of the world. It's the purifying fire by which we start the new season. Maybe you let the Brisbanes and Dohas pass, maybe you missed the opening band, but the Australian Open was never a thing to miss. After all, it was a Grand Slam and there are only four of them and this was the action that would set the circuit in motion, this was what would set the chairs on the stage for the first act. What it typically has not been is a tournament of great surprises. It's not been a clearing of the field, it has been a clarifying of the field, a clarifying *to* the field of the way things are and will be. In a way it's been the kindest of the Grand Slams to me; its scenes of summer and the ebullient blues of the hard courts offer warmth to the spirit and mind during the cold and somber slog through January. Unlike the French Open, Wimbledon, and the U.S. Open, Melbourne gives my mind of winter what it's been missing. I notice it most when in my most inspired moments I want to pick up a racket myself and play; out into the frigid air I go, traveling over the ice, to have a hit on a clay court kept warm under an insulated bubble.

Now it was time to let go of what was and accept what came next. That "accept" bothered me in a way that reminded me of my youth. Something stubborn inside me stirred, and I thought it and then wrote it. Just that word: *accept* . . . it didn't feel like resilience, endurance, or perspective—nor did it feel like what those things should add up to. I had grown up. I had made my peace with the tennis players I grew up with being gone or going. There's a time for all of us. And there's a time to accept that. It's time. Yes, it's time. Lest we fall victim to what ails the world now: nostalgia.

ROGER FEDERER DOES THE BOOGIE

Late at night, New Year's Eve 2016.

Some 2,696 miles away from Brisbane and 2,124 miles away from Melbourne, westward, at the end of the continent right at the shores of the Indian Ocean: Perth, Western Australia, a place referred to by travel writer Bill Bryson as the most remote city on earth. As it approached midnight, somewhere beyond a huge amoeba-shaped fringe of palm-edged pools and the hotel-cum-casino's showy exterior of slanted stacked glass, inside a loud pink-lit ballroom, surrounded by a huge crowd and fifteen fellow tennis players, everyone elbow to elbow, everyone busting a move as the DJ worked the room, Roger Federer was doing the robot on the dance floor.

Andrea Petkovic, one of the game's great bons vivants, had set things off much to the surprise of no one. It had started as one of those event nights. Black-tie, paraded onstage, perfunctory interviews with nice things said nicely, dinner: 495 Australian dollars (A$) for a single ticket; A$900 for what's called a "perfect pair" ticket package, and A$4,500 for a table of ten for "premium West Australian dining and the finest beverages" and a little after-dinner entertainment from Little Bird and DJ Boston Switch to celebrate the start of both 2017 and the twenty-ninth edition of the Hopman Cup.

The Hopman Cup is a mixed-gender exhibition made up of eight teams with two players each, one man and one woman. Like the Davis Cup, Fed Cup, the Olympics, and the Paralympics, it's organized and run by the International Tennis Federation as an event that sorts the players by country, and no ranking points are in play. Federer hadn't played there since 2002 when he was the thirteenth-ranked player in the world, had a total of zero Grand Slams to his name, and his teammate on the Swiss team was Miro-slava "Mirka" Vavrinec. But he hadn't played anywhere, either in an exhibition or official competition, since July, when he blew a late lead and quite literally fell on his face at the Wimbledon semis against Raonic and subsequently canceled the rest of his 2016 schedule in favor, finally, of knee surgery and rest. Sometimes he checked the results as player after player passed him in the rank-ings. By the end of the year, he had dropped to seventeen and he was approaching five years since winning his last Grand Slam tro-phy, and even that one—as he approached thirty-one mired in a two-year title drought—seemed a postscript to the Roger Federer that had been. He kept playing and kept making semifinals, but keeping up with Djokovic on hard courts, Djokovic and Murray at Wimbledon, and the two of them plus Rafa on clay had put a heavy dent in the trophy haul until it eventually came to a halt. In Perth he felt rejuvenated but uncertain about what the future held. So he shrugged his shoulders and danced. Why not? He'd done his homework: week after week of hard training with his team, mainly at his residence in Dubai; this included a live-streamed practice session just nine days ago with the young Frenchman Lucas Pouille. Coincidentally, Pouille, who also lives in Dubai, was one position ahead of Federer now in the rankings and had beaten Nadal at the 2016 U.S. Open. Coincidentally.

Nothing could happen at Brisbane or Dubai that would have been worth the exertion. The seeds were already set for the Australian Open. Federer's seeding would match his rank: seventeenth. If everyone held to form in the Melbourne draw, he would play two qualifiers in the first two rounds . . . and then play the tenth-ranked player in the world in the third . . . and then if he made it past him he'd face the fifth . . . and then Murray in the quarter-finals. Federer never felt he needed much practice to round into shape the way Rafa does, and there was little to be gained from throwing himself right back into the middle of the Murray-Djokovic rivalry at Doha. So why not do something different and return to the Hopman, have some fun, play some doubles with Belinda Bencic, spend some time with the kids on the circuit? Life's short. We have the time we have. He was a kid here once, too: with acne, some leftover teenage grumpiness, and thick shoulder-length hair. Who knows how many opportunities were left to do something like this, when there's no pressure behind you and no expectations ahead? *Nostalgie* in German, *nostalgie* in French, *nostalgia* in English, they all sprout from the same exposed root: the Greek *nostos*—a journey homeward, specifically Odysseus's long voyage home after the end of the Trojan War as told in the *Odyssey*.

Whatever it was, whether it spread from the others there to Federer or from Federer to the others, the atmosphere at the Hopman was unusually amicable. And not just for that night, but something about that night on that dance floor encapsulated the feeling that was in the air. Everyone got up to dance, the players and the folks in the crowd moving in one murmuration. Nick

Kyrgios played it cool before another year betwixt and between the surreal and the sublime. Sascha Zverev, still baby-faced and not yet in the top twenty, played the kid before cracking the top five and picking up a practiced strut along the way. Bencic and Kristina Mladenovic played best friends forever before both of their years flew off the rails as soon as they tasted newfound success. They and the others were going to ring in 2017 right. No hesitation this time, for some reason; they were all in. All of them. Even Dad.

Many of the men had already taken off their jackets and loosened their ties, and Dad Roger Federer was good to go. He looked curated: still dressed in his black tux, his black bow tie still perfectly placed, his jacket still buttoned at the navel, white shirt still perfectly pressed as he moved, the DJ working the room, and the clock counting down the last few minutes of the year. Federer loved the Dad vibe he was giving off, like he was chaperoning the kids on a night at the dance. The players formed an improvised circle around him, shielding him from the bevy of fans who wanted pictures with him, not for his sake—as usual, he was cool with it—but because they thought it was fun to hem him in. And that's when, alone for a moment with the music, he began.

Arms pinned to his sides, elbows slightly bent, stiff in the torso, shoulders back, neck extended as high as it could go—it was a pretty good rendition of the robot. For a few seconds he went off somewhere with the rhythm.

There's a picture you can no doubt find on the Internet that captures this moment. As things circulate across the void they often lose their author, especially now when it's so common that someone takes a picture with someone else's phone and then hands it back to them. Moments are linked now to their subjects rather than their authors. *Mona Lisa* would be an influencer. Daria Gavrilova, Zverev, and Mladenovic are off-center to the right,

Left to right: Roger Federer, unknown, Daria Gavrilova, Alexander "Sascha" Zverev, Kristina "Kiki" Mladenovic. Hopman Cup New Year's Eve Gala, Perth, Australia, December 31, 2016. (Photograph taken by Andrea Petkovic with Daria Gavrilova's phone; courtesy of Andrea Petkovic)

Zverev and Mladenovic leaning into the frame as though they're sneaking into the shot, the shorter Gavrilova standing tall in the center flashing a peace sign with Zverev. Deep in the background on a slight elevation, is the DJ, accompanied, his head down in work, his worktable covered over by a bespectacled man in the middle, jacketless and wearing a red tie, the flash has caught his attention but he doesn't quite know whether to bomb the picture and smile or ignore it, so he just stands there, his indecision leaving behind a pained look on his face. And just ahead of him, to the left of the frame, neither in the foreground nor in the background, Federer is getting his groove on. There's something about it, how everyone is seen and being seen, that still feels fresh and, to be honest, strange. Then again, how could it not be strange: it's a picture of Roger Federer doing the robot framed by people clearly celebrating that they're in a picture in which Roger Federer does the robot. I said it was a pretty good rendition of the robot, but I have to take that back now. It's because of his face. The mouth is wide open and seems as if it has something important to say. And his eyes. Those aren't a robot's eyes. They have too much life in them. He's having too much fun.

FEDERER XVII

Federer's first official match of the year, on the first day of the Australian Open, was unfamiliar territory not only due to the amount of time he had missed but also due to his seeding.

Don't think of a ranking as purely a cosmetic compilation of who's doing well in the circuit and who's not. Rankings also position players in a tournament like pieces on a chessboard. Your ranking has to be high enough to enter a tournament directly, and if you just miss the cut, you get to compete in qualifiers. If you make it through qualifiers, you start from scratch with the rest of the already-qualified field, but having played additional matches and having to play a seeded player.

If you automatically qualify for a tournament but your ranking isn't high enough to receive a seed, then your fate is in the hands of the random draw. Some unseeded players are drawn against other unseeded players, some unseeded players are drawn against a wild card, some unseeded players play a seed. A Grand Slam has a field of 128 players. The first 32 are seeded. So, picture a chart made up of eight sections, and in each of those eight sections picture sixteen players paired up in eight matchups.

Now imagine the top half of the chart being sections 1–4.

And the bottom half of the chart being sections 5–8.

All the matchups in the top half will whittle down the competition until there's only one matchup left. This will be one semifinal. The same thing will happen in the bottom half, yielding one last game in that section: the other semifinal. The winner of the top half of the draw (sections 1–4) will play the winner of the second half of the draw (sections 5–8) in the tournament final. Therefore, certain players can only play each other if they both arrive at the final.

The top two seeds of a tournament are always drawn into separate halves, one in the top and one in the bottom. The idea being that, if everything holds to form, these two players will play in the final. Further, the third seed is put into the other side of the half of the draw that the second seed is in. And the fourth seed is put into the other side of the half of the draw that the first seed is in. The seeding anticipates, again, that if everything holds to form, the third and fourth seeds will be the other semifinalists. The third seed is expected to beat everyone in his or her half of the draw until reaching the second seed. The fourth seed is expected to beat everyone in his or her half of the draw until reaching the first seed. Note that the first seed, as a benefit of being the first seed, is scheduled to play the fourth seed, not the third.

These sections are like ecosystems. The seeding in a section is like the gravity of expectation. When a top seed loses early, all hell breaks loose in a section because a top seed's section consists of players with low seedings, no seedings, wild cards, and qualifiers. Things we call a "Cinderella run" on one side of the coin and "shit shows" on the other occur largely because certain seeds, usually

ROUND 1		ROUND 2	ROUND 3
1. MURRAY, Andy GBR	[1]	A. MURRAY [1]	
2. MARCHENKO, Ilya UKR			A. MURRAY [1]
3. RUBLEV, Andrey RUS	(Q)	A. RUBLEV	
4. LU, Yen-Hsun TPE			
5. DE MINAUR, Alex AUS	(W)	A. DE MINAUR	
6. MELZER, Gerald AUT			S. QUERREY [31]
7. HALYS, Quentin FRA	(W)	S. QUERREY [31]	
8. QUERREY, Sam USA	[31]		
9. ISNER, John USA	[19]	J. ISNER [19]	
10. KRAVCHUK, Konstantin RUS			M. ZVEREV
11. GARCÍA-LÓPEZ, Guillermo ESP		M. ZVEREV	
12. ZVEREV, Mischa GER			
13. JAZIRI, Malek TUN		M. JAZIRI	
14. SOEDA, Go JPN	(Q)		M. JAZIRI
15. BUBLIK, Alexander KAZ	(Q)	A. BUBLIK	
16. POUILLE, Lucas FRA	[16]		
17. BERDYCH, Tomáš CZE	[10]	T. BERDYCH [10]	
18. VANNI, Luca ITA	(Q)		T. BERDYCH [10]
19. HARRISON, Ryan USA		R. HARRISON	
20. MAHUT, Nicolas FRA			
21. FRATANGELO, Bjorn USA	(Q)	N. RUBIN	
22. RUBIN, Noah USA	(Q)		R. FEDERER [17]
23. MELZER, Jürgen AUT	(Q)	R. FEDERER [17]	
24. FEDERER, Roger SUI	[17]		
25. RAMOS-VIÑOLAS, Albert ESP	[26]	L. LACKO	
26. LACKO, Lucáš SVK	(Q)		L. LACKO
27. GRANOLLERS, Marcel ESP		D. SELA	
28. SELA, Dudi ISR			
29. ALMAGRO, Nicolás ESP		J. CHARDY	
30. CHARDY, Jérémy FRA			K. NISHIKORI [5]
31. KUZNETSOV, Andrey RUS		K. NISHIKORI [5]	
32. NISHIKORI, Kei JPN	[5]		
33. WAWRINKA, Stan SUI	[4]	S. WAWRINKA [4]	
34. KLIŽAN, Martin SVK			S. WAWRINKA [4]
35. DELBONIS, Federico ARG		S. JOHNSON	
36. JOHNSON, Steve USA			
37. DUCKWORTH, James AUS		P. LORENZI	
38. LORENZI, Paolo ITA			V. TROICKI [29]
39. DŽUMHUR, Damir BIH		V. TROICKI [29]	
40. TROICKI, Viktor SRB	[29]		
41. CUEVAS, Pablo URU	[22]	D. SCHWARTZMAN	
42. SCHWARTZMAN, Diego ARG			S. DARCIS
43. DARCIS, Steve BEL		S. DARCIS	
44. GROTH, Sam AUS	(W)		
45. MATHIEU, Paul-Henri FRA		A. SEPPI	
46. SEPPI, Andreas ITA			A. SEPPI
47. ELIAS, Gastão POR		N. KYRGIOS [14]	
48. KYRGIOS, Nick AUS	[14]		
49. TSONGA, Jo-Wilfried FRA	[12]	J. TSONGA [12]	
50. MONTEIRO, Thiago BRA			J. TSONGA [12]
51. LAJOVIĆ, Dušan SRB		D. LAJOVIĆ	
52. ROBERT, Stéphane FRA			
53. KHACHANOV, Karen RUS		K. KHACHANOV	
54. MANNARINO, Adrian FRA			J. SOCK [23]
55. HERBERT, Pierre-Hugues FRA		J. SOCK [23]	
56. SOCK, Jack USA	[23]		
57. TOMIC, Bernard AUS	[27]	B. TOMIC [27]	
58. BELLUCCI, Thomaz BRA			B. TOMIC [27]
59. ESTRELLA BURGOS, Victor DOM		V. ESTRELLA BURGOS	
60. BEDENE, Aljaž GBR			
61. BAGNIS, Facundo ARG		D. EVANS	
62. EVANS, Daniel GBR			D. EVANS
63. JANOWICZ, Jerzy POL		M. ČILIĆ [7]	
64. ČILIĆ, Marin CRO	[7]		

AUSTRALIAN OPEN
2017 MEN'S SINGLES

A. MURRAY [1]

M. ZVEREV

M. ZVEREV

R. FEDERER [17]

R. FEDERER [17]

R. FEDERER [17]

K. NISHIKORI [5]

S. WAWRINKA [4]

S. WAWRINKA [4]

A. SEPPI

R. FEDERER [17]

J. TSONGA [12]

S. WAWRINKA [4]

J. TSONGA [12]

D. EVANS

Champion:
FEDERER, Roger SUI

ROUND 1		ROUND 2	ROUND 3
65. MONFILS, Gaël FRA	[6]	G. MONFILS [6]	
66. VESELÝ, Jiří CZE			G. MONFILS [6]
67. DOLGOPOLOV, Alexandr UKR		A. DOLGOPOLOV	
68. ĆORIĆ, Borna CRO			
69. FABBIANO, Thomas ITA	(Q)	D. YOUNG	
70. YOUNG, Donald USA			P. KOHLSCHREIBER [32]
71. BASILASHVILI, Nikoloz GEO		P. KOHLSCHREIBER [32]	
72. KOHLSCHREIBER, Philipp GER	[32]		
73. ZVEREV, Alexander GER	[24]	A. ZVEREV [24]	
74. HAASE, Robin NED			A. ZVEREV [24]
75. TIAFOE, Frances USA	(Q)	F. TIAFOE	
76. KUKUSHKIN, Mikhail KAZ			
77. YOUZHNY, Mikhail RUS		M. BAGHDATIS	
78. BAGHDATIS, Marcos CYP			R. NADAL [9]
79. MAYER, Florian GER		R. NADAL [9]	
80. NADAL, Rafael ESP	[9]		
81. BAUTISTA AGUT, Roberto ESP	[13]	R. BAUTISTA AGUT [13]	
82. PELLA, Guido ARG			R. BAUTISTA AGUT [13]
83. NISHIOKA, Yoshihito JPN		Y. NISHIOKA	
84. BOLT, Alex AUS	(Q)		
85. MEDVEDEV, Daniil RUS		E. ESCOBEDO	
86. ESCOBEDO, Ernesto USA	(Q)		D. FERRER [21]
87. JASIKA, Omar AUS	(W)	D. FERRER [21]	
88. FERRER, David ESP	[21]		
89. SIMON, Gilles FRA	[25]	G. SIMON [25]	
90. MMOH, Michael USA	(W)		G. SIMON [25]
91. DONALDSON, Jared USA		R. DUTRA SILVA	
92. DUTRA SILVA, Rogério BRA			
93. MÜLLER, Gilles LUX		G. MÜLLER	
94. FRITZ, Taylor USA			M. RAONIC [3]
95. BROWN, Dustin GER		M. RAONIC [3]	
96. RAONIC, Milos CAN	[3]		
97. THIEM, Dominic AUT	[8]	D. THIEM [8]	
98. STRUFF, Jan-Lennard GER			D. THIEM [8]
99. THOMPSON, Jordan AUS		J. THOMPSON	
100. SOUSA, João POR			
101. HAAS, Tommy GER		B. PAIRE	
102. PAIRE, Benoît FRA			B. PAIRE
103. FOGNINI, Fabio ITA		F. FOGNINI	
104. LÓPEZ, Feliciano ESP	[28]		
105. KARLOVIĆ, Ivo CRO	[20]	I. KARLOVIĆ [20]	
106. ZEBALLOS, Horacio ARG			I. KARLOVIĆ [20]
107. PAVLÁSEK, Adam CZE		A. WHITTINGTON	
108. WHITTINGTON, Andrew AUS	(W)		
109. TURSUNOV, Dmitry RUS		R. ŠTĚPÁNEK	
110. ŠTĚPÁNEK, Radek CZE	(Q)		D. GOFFIN [11]
111. OPELKA, Reilly USA	(Q)	D. GOFFIN [11]	
112. GOFFIN, David BEL	[11]		
113. DIMITROV, Grigor BUL	[15]	G. DIMITROV [15]	
114. O'CONNELL, Christopher AUS	(W)		G. DIMITROV [15]
115. CHUNG, Hyeon KOR		H. CHUNG	
116. OLIVO, Renzo ARG			
117. ALBOT, Radu MDA		C. BERLOCQ	
118. BERLOCQ, Carlos ARG			R. GASQUET [18]
119. MOTT, Blake AUS	(Q)	R. GASQUET [18]	
120. GASQUET, Richard FRA	[18]		
121. CARREÑO BUSTA, Pablo ESP	[30]	P. CARREÑO BUSTA [30]	
122. POLANSKY, Peter CAN	(L)		P. CARREÑO BUSTA [30]
123. EDMUND, Kyle GBR		K. EDMUND	
124. GIRALDO, Santiago COL			
125. ISTOMIN, Denis UZB	(W)	D. ISTOMIN	
126. DODIG, Ivan CRO	(Q)		D. ISTOMIN
127. VERDASCO, Fernando ESP		N. DJOKOVIC [2]	
128. DJOKOVIC, Novak SRB	[2]		

ROUND 4　　　　QUARTERFINALS　　　　SEMIFINALS

G. MONFILS [6]

R. NADAL [9]

R. NADAL [9]

R. NADAL [9]

R. BAUTISTA AGUT [13]

M. RAONIC [3]

M. RAONIC [3]

R. NADAL [9]

D. THIEM [8]

D. GOFFIN [11]

D. GOFFIN [11]

G. DIMITROV [15]

G. DIMITROV [15]

G. DIMITROV [15]

D. ISTOMIN

the very top ones, get knocked out of their section early. Sometimes, though, an unseeded player or a wild card could mean trouble for everyone else in a section of the entire draw. In 2007, Serena Williams returned to tennis after some time away engaging in other pursuits. She entered the Australian Open ranked eighty-first in the world and therefore unseeded. She landed in a section of the draw in which the top dog was fifth-seeded Nadia Petrova. Unlucky, Nadia. The top seed was Maria Sharapova. Suffice it to say, Serena won that tournament.

You can easily see how all this gets turned on its head, but the general idea is that as the pairings reduce in number, the higher seeds survive. It goes by quickly: a section of one half of the draw of a Grand Slam begins with sixteen players, by the second round it's down to eight, by the third round four, and by the fourth round only two players are left. The winner of a fourth-round match is the winner of that section. The winner of that section is what a quarterfinalist is. The top eight seeds are the heads of the tables of the eight sections of the tournament and therefore the players, by logic of their seeding, who are expected to make it to the quarterfinals. How they are paired up is a matter of the random chance of the draw.

Simple enough. I just wanted to lay this all out so we can keep in mind how screwed Roger Federer was at the start of the Australian Open as the seventeenth seed. Simply by looking at the draw again, you see Scylla and Charybdis waiting all over the place. He was going to have to get past Tomáš Berdych, the tenth seed and tenth-ranked player in the world, just for the pleasure of playing the fifth seed and fifth-ranked Nishikori. Beating Nishikori after beating Berdych would win him the section and leave him with, in theory, a quarterfinal matchup with Murray. If he beat Berdych, Nishikori, and world number one Murray, who was 28–1 in his last 29 matches, he would play Wawrinka, who just won the last U.S. Open over Djokovic and beat Nadal in 2014 in Melbourne. And if he beat Berdych, Nishikori, Murray, and Wawrinka, he would get for his troubles a final against Djokovic, whom he hadn't beaten in a Grand Slam match since the 2012 Wimbledon semifinal.

Add to this the fact that you can't even assume as the seventeenth seed making it past the qualifier in the first round. A qualifier may not be as good as a seed, and is all but guaranteed to run out of gas if lucky enough to win a few rounds. But in the first round a qualifier can be an extremely tricky opponent, because by the time a qualifier arrives at the first round of a tournament that player is game-ready, battle-tested, and on a winning streak. While the seeded player was going through the motions at practice or a promotional event, the qualifier was scrapping on the court for prize money that to him actually matters. And sometimes a wild card shows up who's completely off the radar and throws a player out of whack.

In the first round of the 2016 Australian Open, the seventeenth seed in the men's singles field was Benoît Paire. He played a nineteen-year-old wild card from Long Island named Noah Rubin, a small and scrappy player who had recently turned pro after playing a year of college tennis at Wake Forest and was ranked 328th in the world. Rubin scraped and clawed his way through the first set by winning the tiebreak, 7–4. Then he batted enough balls back at a bemused Paire to win the second set in a tiebreak, 8–6. It was Benoît-breaks-racket time. He lost the third set in another tiebreak, 7–5. "Not much to say except it was a catastrophe," Paire said after the match. That and that Rubin was "not a very good player."

Rubin went on to lose his next match in Melbourne in straight sets to qualifier Pierre-Hugues Herbert of France, who breezed past him in the first two sets before bageling him in the third and final set. Herbert went on to lose in the third round to his countryman Jo-Wilfried Tsonga, the ninth seed, in three close sets, including tight tiebreakers in the final two. Tsonga then went on to lose in the fourth round to the seventh-seed Nishikori in straight sets, who then lost to Djokovic in the quarterfinals in straight sets. The chain of losing set off by seventeenth-seeded Paire in section two of the top half of the draw was finally put to pasture by Djokovic in the semifinals gliding by the third seed, Roger Federer.

Of course, Roger Federer isn't Benoît Paire, an exquisite talent capable of losing the plot at any moment and, that not being sufficient for someone so skilled at losing the plot, who can then proceed to lose the plot of having lost the plot. The fact remained, though, that to be seeded seventeen was to be dropped down into the middle of a dark woods. Seventeen was going to have to be good to him. Then again, it already had been, hadn't it? It was exactly the number of Grand Slam titles he'd won.

REBIRTH: ROUND ONE

Playing in a Grand Slam at thirty-five, after a long layoff and with his top-ten ranking a thing of the past, Federer seemed to take the first-round draw he received in stride. Everyone on the circuit is younger than him, or at least it feels that way. Okay, Feliciano López isn't younger than him. They go all the way back to juniors: the Orange Bowl in 1998—they were there, Andy Roddick, David Nalbandian, and Guillermo "El Mago" Coria, too. Those last three are already retired. And have been for a while.

Now, sometimes what comes with hearing "1998" isn't a flashback to that tournament in Florida for the best-of-the-best juniors, but rather a wide-eyed wild card or qualifier saying to him now, "Oh, wow, 1998: that was the year I was born."

At some point Federer started to take for granted that, in order to keep competing at this level, he was going to have to think of his age. Play quick, attack, attack some more, keep the points short, stay as fresh as possible this way. At his age and coming off an injury layoff, there wasn't going to be a Plan B. All of that rehabilitation and the long preparation of the body and mind for a moment in Melbourne that could be ruefully short or unexpectedly long, a Cinderella run. The last time they played, he won. And in straight sets, no less. They were in Monte Carlo that day, on red clay in the quarterfinals. That was six seasons ago, though. The plan was straightforward, as at his age and with so much rust on the legs it needed to be. The plan wasn't going to be a surprise; he'd been around for so long it wasn't going to be a secret how he would want to play. He reminded himself: play fast; be as aggressive as possible on the backhand; hit it with bad intentions, always; and find his backhand, especially on the key points. They had played before on big stages, all in one flash—Wimbledon, 2010 round of sixteen; New York, 2010 round of sixteen; the quarters of the indoor Masters 1000 in Paris, also in 2010—each match an improvement before the triumph in Monte Carlo. He could hang the baseball cap he played in on that. Plus, the fact that at least for this match he took away from him the mantle of old soul. Jürgen Melzer was born in May 1981, ten weeks before Roger Federer.

The first set would slip away from him 5–7, but he was solidly in the match. As they warmed up before the match, hitting balls casually back and forth to each other, Federer hit four balls in a row with the frame instead of the strings. They'd known each other for a long time, the thirty-five-year-old Austrian and the thirty-five-year-old Swiss, and had hit balls back and forth to each other going all the way back to that Orange Bowl in the last millennium. By this point in their careers they knew both nervousness and rust when they saw them. And they saw it in each other—easy shots sailing long due to surges of adrenaline; the body too refreshed and chipper to be properly game-ready. What were they going to do about it?

For Melzer's part, he used his lefty two-handed backhand, which he hits with tremendous body torque, to hustle the ball deep into the corners, the idea being that such balls would push his opponent back. But Federer, for better and for worse, refused. He stayed on the baseline and flicked those shots back, taking them on the short hop, quickly and with minimal swing. He missed some, but kept going after them, and he hit enough of them to throw Melzer's timing off when he'd thought he'd hit a winner or set himself up to win the point with one more stroke but instead would see a winner fly past him. Still, Melzer held course, sensed an opening in Federer's high-risk approach, and pushed hard when he had made some headway in Federer's service games. Melzer won the second set 6–3. Federer won the next two sets by identical scores of 6–2.

Melzer played craftily, letting his left-handedness mix and match with Federer's patterns for playing points. The push and pull of a left-handed topspin forehand followed by an extremely flat, lefty two-handed backhand, that type of inside-out game Melzer put on display, reminded me a little bit of Nadal, though there's no comparison, as Nadal is incomparable. And besides, the days were long gone of the two of them looking over the draw to see who was in the way of the inevitable. Still, Nadal was on the other side of the draw, though—the ninth seed, in Gaël Monfils's section of the draw—which meant that the only way they would play would be if both reached the . . . Never mind. The next match in two days' time would be with none other than Rubin, who qualified this time around and beat another qualifier to book his place in the second round. Rest was what was important now, and the rest was silence. After the match, Federer wondered aloud how many times the first round has not been easy—almost every time, he said. I couldn't help but notice how he phrased the sentence: he left out the hard words, the ones that spread their roots in the mind—*difficult, hard*—no, the first round has a habit of not being easy. In the beginning, the mind paints layer after layer of possible futures. The present scrubs all of them and leaves one. The words we use, then, to speak of it become so important. And so choosing your words wisely is a way of saying to that painter in your head, *Let there be light.*

RAFAEL NADAL FIGHTS THE GODS

On the second day of the Australian Open, Nadal also beat an older player, thirty-three-year-old Florian Mayer, 6–3, 6–4, 6–4. He served extraordinarily well. Over his career his serve has been the one part of his game that wasn't at the level of the rest. He knew how to make use of the left-handed angles to his advantage, but his serve was more a point-starter than anything else. Part of what started to separate Djokovic and Murray from him had been their relentless aggression in returning the Nadal serve, as he wasn't one to hit it past you, or even really try to.

In recent years, however, this had turned into a recipe for disaster against Novak and Andy. Even on clay, where he'd recently lost to Murray in Madrid and Djokovic at Roland-Garros, his Batcave and his Fortress of Solitude. He had a new coach in his box with his uncle, Toni Nadal, who had been his one and only coach since he first started to play. Now fellow Mallorcan and former world number one Carlos Moyá, a longtime friend, was part of the team.

The Nadal circle is famous for being small, tight, and familial. Hence, the ideas that have circulated through it for years have been in-house ideas. While Moyá wasn't exactly a stranger, he had observed Nadal's game from outside that circle and was one of the very few people, perhaps even the only person, capable of introducing solutions from the exterior that would be heeded and, possibly, adopted. Improving the serve, making it more of a weapon rather than just a tool, became a mission.

Mayer was the first player in 2017 to truly bear the brunt of it. The numbers tell a brutal story: six aces, which is somewhat high for Nadal, don't really stand out; but then there was the 70 percent first-serve percentage; the 77 percent of first serves won; the remarkable 83 percent of second-serve points won; and not a single break point faced. It was a trend that would continue for the year. Advanced tennis ratings system Peak Serve Elo calculated that Nadal was the most improved server of 2017 by a remarkable distance over the second most improved, Dolgopolov, who after losing to Nadal in Brisbane would rebound strongly as the year went on.

Nadal was embracing attack mode, starting with the serve. The draw also looked promising. He was in section five in the bottom half of the draw. Monfils, the sixth seed, had played brilliantly in the second half of 2016 and closed out that year with a career-high ranking of six. No one played the game like Monfils: When he was on his game, it was like watching a star go nova on the court. But after such bursts, he always waned. Though his title haul was meager compared to his gifts, he enjoyed a rich, successful life on the circuit. And yet, the lingering feeling followed him that he was capable of more. He, Nadal, Djokovic, and Murray are separated in age by less than a year, and it was Monfils who was the star among stars when they were juniors. There was no cap on his talent. In 2004, he was the number-one-ranked junior in the world and won the boys' singles at the Australian Open, the French Open, and Wimbledon. He was seventeen years old. On the professional circuit, his combined record against the triumvirate of

Nadal, Djokovic, and Murray stood at four wins and thirty-one losses. None of those four wins had come against Djokovic, who still points out in post-match interviews after beating him that in juniors Monfils was "the man." Nadal's record against him was twelve wins in fourteen matches. If there was a player at the top of one of the sections of the draw who would be particularly vulnerable in the fourth round, it was Monfils. Even Monfils had to know it, which was even better for Nadal. Let him think about it.

Monfils beats Jiří Veselý in the first round, 6–2, 6–3, 6–2.

Nadal beats Marcos Baghdatis in the second round, 6–3, 6–1, 6–3.

Let him think about it.

Monfils beats Dolgopolov, 6–3, 6–4, 1–6, 6–0. (On set point in a closely disputed second frame Monfils plays one ball from behind his back, coaxing a forehand into the net by Dolgopolov.)

Nadal does a classic rope-a-dope comeback on young Sascha Zverev to the tune of 4–6, 6–3, 6–7 (7–5), 6–3, 6–2.

Let him think about it.

Monfils beats Philipp Kohlschreiber in the third round, 6–3, 7–6 (7–1), 6–4. (With Monfils serving for the first set at 5–3, Kohlschreiber lobs a volley over the head of Monfils, who had ghosted into the net, causing him to chase the ball back to the baseline, turn, and, for some inexplicable reason, pirouette into the air as he turned to hit a forehand back to Kohlschreiber, who, standing at the net and left with the simple task of blocking the ball back into the empty court, flinches, as though he's just seen a ghost, and dumps the easiest of volleys directly into the net.) Monfils isn't thinking about it. If there's ever been a play-the-person-in-front-of-you player, it's Gaël Monfils. That he wasn't thinking about Nadal is part of his strength. But also, maybe, part of his weakness. One doesn't simply walk into a Rafa Nadal match.

And so a Monfils-Nadal fourth round beckoned, the sixth seed against the ninth. Zero Grand Slam titles versus fourteen. Monfils, reborn on the court, was looking to go deep in his second straight Grand Slam tournament after making the semifinals in New York. He was the higher-ranked player and on the best run of his career. But he'd lost five straight matches to players in the top ten. He thought about it.

By this point, Djokovic had been knocked out by Istomin, and now, on their day off, Monfils and Nadal would get wind of the fact that Murray had lost to Sascha Zverev's older brother, Mischa. And that Federer had knocked out Nishikori. Things continued in that vein the day of their match when David Goffin defeated the eighth-seeded Dominic Thiem. Thus, as night approached and Nadal's match inched closer, the draw had opened up like a nocturnal flower. Raonic was the highest seed left. Federer might have just used up all he had left in the tank getting by Nishikori in five sets. Mischa Zverev wasn't going to beat Roger after beating Andy. Suddenly Federer looked less like a novel return to the tour and more like a legitimate threat. At least he and Wawrinka, the 2014 Australian Open champion here and winner of the last Grand Slam, would cancel each other out in the semifinal— only one could get by. On Monfils's side of the draw, aside from the great former champion Nadal, only players from that tween generation remained. Raonic, Goffin, Dimitrov: the kids hyped as the next great things who've settled into being pretty good but certainly not great and aren't kids anymore. Monfils doesn't think about them. That he can take them. That he can handle anyone left in the draw. That if he comes out for the last match of the evening and plays the perfect version of his tennis and makes things difficult for Nadal, then maybe, just maybe . . . Melbourne's nice.

After giving the first two sets away with minimal resistance, Monfils recovers to take the third, only to go on to lose to Nadal

3–6, 3–6, 6–4, 4–6. Afterward, his ranking dropped week after week without end. The fourth round became a wall that he could not pass: he managed to do so only three times all year. He withdrew from six tournaments due to injury or ailment. On the last day of 2017, he was ranked forty-sixth. He had started the year ranked seventh. And if you haven't seen the match, and want to know more than who won, what can 6–3, 6–3, 4–6, 6–4 mean to you? The 4–2 lead Monfils enjoyed in the fourth as Nadal looked frustrated and out of gas? The three straight unforced errors Monfils made as he was serving to stay in the match? We take these things as empirical evidence. These are things that Gaël Monfils does. And things that Rafa Nadal does. Where once there were liquid bends in the course of a player's career, all the little things gather and crystallize into diamond-hard formations, truths we settle for as part of the deal of getting involved with sports in the first place. Once upon a time at the end of 2016, Gaël Monfils had risen to sixth in the rankings and was finally playing the best tennis of his life. He came into 2017 in great form and the results at the Australian Open were falling his way. Then you stop and wonder why things turn the way they do. How some players constantly ride the current to their particular embankment of the stream time and time again, then get off at that embankment until the current comes back for them again. Come summer, Monfils will lose at Wimbledon in the third round, which is as far as he's ever gone, for the sixth time in his career. At the start of 2018 he'll storm through a depleted field in Doha for his seventh title. At some point you'll be curious again about Rafa Nadal's journey to the 2017 Australian Open final, which you'll consider a kind of secular resurrection. You'll look at the numbers for his match with Monfils and see 6–3, 6–3, 4–6, 6–4. It will be enough to convince you that was all there was. It is what it is.

The truth is, there was no possible end to the 2017 Australian Open that would not have made a story for the ages. Venus Williams at thirty-six winning her first major in nine years. Serena Williams at thirty-four returning to top form, winning her open-era record twenty-third major title and reclaiming the number-one ranking. Roger Federer at thirty-five winning an improbable eighteenth major title in his first competitive tournament after a sixth-month self-imposed hiatus due to injury and against no less than his one true rival. Rafa Nadal, at thirty, and who in recent seasons had seemed gnawed on by Father Time with all the guilty, wide-eyed ravenousness of Goya's *Saturn Devouring His Son*, unexpectedly capturing his fifteenth major title, edging a mere two major titles away from Federer's record total and, coupled with a 24–11 head-to-head record against Federer, emphatically making his strongest claim yet to being the greatest player the men's tour had ever seen.

Every possible outcome would have hit some sweet spot, that part of you that flutters and pinwheels and is hard to reckon with and hard to reconcile, the nostalgia of the cynic, the romance buried in the hard-hearted, that something in you that makes you feel like Pluto was the ninth planet again and because of it, though still the same rock, sang sweeter in the music of the spheres than it had ever sung before. This technocracy we find ourselves living in trying our best to be actual people makes time seem to pass so quickly, the length of an era shrinking to the duration of the attention span of an impatient child. Perhaps this past weekend at the Australian Open was less a passing chance to remember your younger self and cheer the all-conquering versions of Venus, Roger, Serena, and Rafa's younger selves, and more an opportunity to remember how quickly these moments we have—all of us—to define ourselves pass us by. And how thin the margins in those moments can be.

For example, serving with advantage, up 3–2 in the fifth set and cooking with the momentum of not only having won the fourth set 6–3 but having opened this deciding fifth set by breaking his opponent, Rafa Nadal looked poised to pestle Roger Federer down in yet another final. He had already done it twenty-three of the thirty-four times the two had played overall, and nine times out of the eleven they had faced each other in the four major tournaments. No player had won as much as Federer. But no player had caused him to suffer like Nadal had. Both players had had their on moments and their off moments, and now the match had seemed to capture its intended rhythm, the familiar one: game, set, match—Nadal.

But tennis is a game of undulating rhythms that exist in four concentric circles—the rhythm of a point, the rhythm of a service game, the rhythm of a return game, the rhythm of a set—that are interrelated but don't necessarily touch. Sometimes you can see them simply in the scoreline: 4–6, 6–3, 1–6, 6–3, 3–2. Advantage Nadal. Like an idea of order.

The two first played in 2004 in Miami, when seventeen-year-old and thirty-fourth-ranked Nadal sent ripples through the tennis world by defeating the top-ranked Federer, then twenty-three, in straight sets. Since then they have faced each other on hard courts and clay courts, quick courts and slow courts, half-clay and half-grass courts, Dubai courts and Cincinnati courts, for better and for worse, in sickness and in health.

Nadal's advantages in the matchup have largely been physiological: his thumping left-handed topspin forehand had spent the better part of a decade grinding down on Federer's right-handed and, crucially, one-handed backhand. The deep, high-bouncing ball is the one-handed backhand's structural flaw, like that blind spot in any car's rearview mirror. It's extremely difficult to generate pace hitting a high one-handed backhand. And Nadal, like Navratilova and McEnroe before him, has crafted his left-handedness into an art. Nadal's natural crosscourt forehand from the left side just so happens to be a menace to Federer's natural backhand motion. But it's not just that Nadal is left-handed; it's that, unlike most lefties, his game is a mosaic of stroke patterns designed to take advantage of what in Latin and still in Spanish would be known as his sinister side. If Federer's looping, elegant, artisanal one-handed backhand off the right side has been the cobra of the ATP Tour, Nadal's quick, torquing, relentless forehand has been the mongoose.

But it turns out that Federer, after so many years of encountering the same problem, did bring a surprise with him into this final: he had altered his backhand. Suddenly he was hitting it flatter. Much flatter. You could see the difference on the shot off the racket, you could see the difference in his follow-through; it was curter—the high curlicue finish of the racket with a twist of the wrist was gone . . . he swung the backhand now more like someone opening a stuck door.

And he all but abandoned the backhand slice. Both the topspin one-handed backhand and the backhand slice are lifesavers: they give the person playing them a chance to get back into the point by slowing the pace of the ball and altering the pace of the point, the change in the bounce also changing the swing trajectory of the opponent. Nadal, however, being no ordinary opponent, tends to use these attempts at changing the pace to instead find the pace he desires, and the low, skidding bounce of a slice, especially crosscourt from a right-hander, slots perfectly into the exaggerated low approach in the swing of his forehand. Ironically, Federer's attempts to save himself in a point by using the topspin and slice often led to his long-term demise in these face-offs. Nadal knew it and feasted off it. Federer knew it as well, and yet he seemed to be unable to adjust. The strength of the one-handed backhand to viewers is its aesthetic appeal, but to a player its strength lies in its flexibility. It is an easier stroke through which both to master and disguise variations of spin. And unless you're Nicolás Almagro, Richard Gasquet, Stan Wawrinka, or Dominic Thiem—the Four Horsemen of the One-Handed Backhand—there's not much you can do off that wing with a one-hander when you're pushed to the back of the court other than slice the ball back. And that would be more of the same meal for Nadal to feast on.

So Federer, possibly taking cues from Grigor Dimitrov's electric semifinal performance against Nadal, decided to swing hard, almost without fail, swing hard and flat and go at Rafa's forehand. It bore fruit for Federer in the first and third sets, but the second and fourth were near mirror images of each other, with Federer's own forehand, considered widely the greatest shot in the history of tennis, letting him down repeatedly.

And so here they were now, the one secret played between the two longtime rivals now out in the open. Nadal had had four sets to adjust to Federer's backhand adjustment and the match seems now to have stabilized back to the way they tended to go: 4–6, 6–3, 1–6, 6–3, 3–2, having just crushed a short forehand winner down the line off a soft Federer return served as wide as possible to his backhand side the last time Nadal had him in the ad court, and now Nadal has him on the ad side again—one point from 4–2 and a vise grip on the match—as he leans forward at the baseline, fidgets with one shoulder, then the other, touches one side of his nose, then the other, then the other, pushes aside his hair, then picks at his shorts from the back before beginning the motion of his serve.

The point total at this very moment of the match: Federer, 131; Nadal, 131.

As Nadal, mid-serve, stares up at the ball above his head, he will never be closer to winning this match than at that very moment just before he springs up and forward as his Babolat racket smacks at the toss.

Remember that part just before about Nadal's tried-and-trusted patterns against Federer, including that wide serve to the backhand? Well, so did Nadal. And so did Federer. Maybe. Maybe not? But Nadal banked on knowing that Federer knew that Nadal knew. Suffice it to say, Nadal tried to surprise Federer with a body serve and Federer on reflex blocked the ball back and it tumbled, slow and lob-like, crosscourt and deep into the corner it came from. Federer, completely on the defensive now, has at least bought himself some time, which he uses to reposition himself at the center of the baseline. All he can do now is wait. The game is on Nadal's racket now. The ball tamely hangs in the air. He decides to go for the kill. Now comes the wide shot he passed up on the serve. It was a classic cat-and-mouse game within the service game. The body serve coaxed a defensive reply from Federer and he recovered to the middle of the court, as he should. A lane for a short crosscourt winner opened up, a shot tailor-made for Nadal's lefty topspin forehand. Nadal goes for it and it clips the tape on the top of the net. But the topspin Nadal hits with doesn't allow the unforced error to die a quick death, no, it pops and remainders down to a spot on the court close enough to seem that it might possibly fall in but in the end far enough out to be without question out on first glance.

Forty–all now. Total points: 132 Federer, 131 Nadal.

The next point is a rapid-fire five-shot slugfest that Federer ends emphatically with a flat backhand crosscourt winner from the ad side. (Eight of Federer's fourteen backhand winners come in the final set of the match.) Advantage Federer. The break comes shortly

RANKING	MOVE	PLAYER	AGE	POINTS	TOURN PLAYED	POINTS DROPPING
1	–	Andy Murray	29	11,540	17	0
2	–	Novak Djokovic	29	9,825	17	0
3	^1	Stan Wawrinka	31	5,695	21	0
4	v1	Milos Raonic	26	4,930	19	0
5	–	Kei Nishikori	27	4,830	20	0
6	^3	Rafael Nadal	30	4,385	16	0
7	–	Marin Čilić	28	3,560	22	0
8	–	Dominic Thiem	23	3,505	28	0
9	v3	Gaël Monfils	30	3,445	18	0
10	^7	Roger Federer	35	3,260	14	0
11	–	David Goffin	26	2,930	24	0
12	v2	Tomáš Berdych	31	2,790	21	0
13	^2	Grigor Dimitrov	25	2,765	24	0
14	v2	Jo-Wilfried Tsonga	31	2,685	17	0
15	v2	Nick Kyrgios	21	2,415	20	0
16	v2	Roberto Bautista Agut	28	2,350	24	0
17	v1	Lucas Pouille	22	2,131	24	0
18	–	Richard Gasquet	30	1,975	20	0
19	^2	Ivo Karlović	37	1,875	24	0
20	–	Jack Sock	24	1,855	19	0

Official ATP Rankings, January 30, 2017. (www.atpworldtour.com)

after, Nadal spraying an inside-out forehand from the deuce side wide at the end of another hard exchange of groundstrokes. Nadal is broken: 3–all in the fifth now. Nadal never wins another game. He'll win eight more points for the rest of the match: 4–6, 6–3, 1–6, 6–3, 3–6. But it was closer than that. It was much, much closer than that. They say baseball is a game of inches. A discussion that could have lasted a lifetime—who is the greatest male tennis player you've ever seen—was ended by a quarter-centimeter of braided net cord as the world turned.

March, and the middle ground between winter and spring. The Australian Open recedes into the past, and on the near horizon ahead, red as the setting sun, you can already see a hint of the clay-court season. But first the circuit stops in the United States for an early and rather short stay for what's commonly called the Sunshine Swing through the American hard courts: there's the stop in Key Biscayne and before that at the more prestigious BNP Paribas Open, known casually by the name of the small fifty-year-old resort town in the Coachella Valley where it takes place—Indian Wells, California.

I flew in from New York for the men's and women's quarterfinals and decided to stay for the rest. And as I watched the tennis press feverishly filing match reports and injury updates, and tweeting about whatever nuggets they could unearth during press conferences, I wondered what it would be like to write—how shall I put it—off the beat, out of sync, out of time. I have a friend, a distinguished historian, who goes out of his way to keep his comments on current events to the bare minimum. He thinks it takes fifteen to twenty years before we really know what any happening actually was. Gregarious and outspoken by nature, he shows a different self when the news of the moment comes up among friends and colleagues. This is when he tends to let others do the talking, for the most part chiming in with a "We won't know for a long time what was going on" or "That seems to be what happened, but we don't know yet what it means" or, particularly when the hot takes start flying around, "Meh."

With apologies to the Western & Southern Open in Cincinnati, Indian Wells is the second great American showcase of tennis. The

BNP Paribas Open is a Masters 1000 event on the men's ATP World Tour (one of eight such on the ATP) and a "Premier Mandatory" event on the women's WTA Tour (one of four). After the four majors—the Australian Open, the French Open, Wimbledon, and the U.S. Open—and the end-of-the-year ATP World Tour Finals (a specialized tournament specifically for the top eight players), these Masters 1000s and Premier Mandatory tournaments are the next big thing. And among them all, Indian Wells has managed to distinguish itself: it draws more spectators than any tennis tournament outside the four majors, and among permanent tennis stadiums only New York's Arthur Ashe is larger than the Indian Wells Tennis Garden's 16,100-seat main stadium. The tournament is casually referred to in tennis circles as the fifth major. This is noteworthy in no small part because the four majors are long-standing celebrations of the metropolis, while Indian Wells was incorporated into a city just fifty years ago and the 2010 U.S. Census put its population at 4,958 inhabitants. Tech billionaire Larry Ellison bought the tournament and the grounds on which it takes place in 2009 for $100 million. Since then it has grown—bejeweling itself with such trappings of wealth and lavishness that approach rivaling tennis's temple to consumerism, the U.S. Open. This includes sprawling versions of both Spago and Nobu on the grounds, the former with table-side views of the main court. Both restaurants are open for just the two weeks of the tournament.

If you compare the size of the main stadium to the size of the city, it quickly becomes clear to you that the tournament is a destination event. I was struck by the number of people in the place who walked around the area—which includes Palm Desert and Palm Springs—with rackets and racket bags. They were at the airport, on the streets, loaded up in cars, gathered in hotel lobbies, and on the grounds themselves, where they could take lessons or

even get a game in on one of the practice courts. It is a Shangri-la for the tennis weekend warrior and the tennis-loving retiree. It dawned on me that the city is a tour stop as much for the fans as for the players themselves, that the interest shared between fans and players here reaches the peak of shared intensity. In this sense, the tournament at Indian Wells is a mirror of its community, or at least the community it most wants to project out to the world: unlike the great urban tournaments, Indian Wells is a celebration of the sporty resort and of the way of life that keeps it running; tennis being both flattering mirror and stage for performers who play the roles of younger, better-playing versions of the audience.

Maybe this was at the root of the 2001 crowd turning so savagely and unfairly on the Williams family. That year, Venus and Serena were to play each other in one of the women's semifinals at Indian Wells. But, citing a case of tendonitis in her knee, Venus pulled out of the match four minutes before it was set to begin. This led to a tremendous amount of outrage that culminated in the fifteen-thousand-person crowd for the women's final showering a continual torrent of abuse at Serena on the court and their family, including Venus, in the stands. It was a bad enough situation for both sisters to boycott Indian Wells from 2002 to 2015. For all of the sport's beauty and grace, the perfume of Narcissus exudes from tennis crowds at matches of this level.

Confetti after the men's singles final at the BNP Paribas Open, Indian Wells, California. (Courtesy of the author)

They tend to love what they see when they can think that, if they squint long and hard enough, they see themselves. And the epitome of this is Roger Federer.

When Roger Federer plays a tennis match, the questions are almost all about Roger. And when Roger Federer doesn't play a tennis match, the questions are almost all about Roger. At Indian Wells, I was witness to this up close, and words fail to explain the phenomena. I worry for any tennis pro armed with high aspirations and the initials R.F., because he or she will no doubt end up facing four to five questions per match about how they handle the pressure of having the same initials as Roger Federer, if they asked Roger for advice on having the initials R.F., and if a name change was ever under consideration.

No player has suffered the slings and arrows of Not-Being-Roger more than his Swiss compatriot Stan Wawrinka. Just before Stan stepped foot onto the court for his quarterfinal match at Indian Wells, ESPN's Pam Shriver wanted to ask him an important question: Had he seen Federer's demolition of Rafa Nadal the night before? Wawrinka had to remind Shriver that, no, he in fact didn't see Federer play . . . because he himself was playing on another court at the same time. Shriver, a former player who spent her long career in the shadow of Martina Navratilova and Chris Evert, was somehow neither unbowed nor empathetic: she followed up with another question about Federer. Wawrinka is a three-time major champion, having won the Australian Open in 2014, the French Open in 2015, and the U.S. Open in 2016. And none of those wins came via a fortuitous draw: he had to get through Djokovic and Nadal at the 2014 Australian Open, Federer and Djokovic at the 2015 French Open, and resurgent 2009 U.S. Open champion Juan Martín del Potro, 2014 U.S. Open runner-up Kei Nishikori (who had just beaten Andy Murray in the previous round), and Djokovic again at the 2016 U.S. Open.

If Wawrinka wins Wimbledon he will attain the extremely rare career Grand Slam; to put this in perspective, Andy Murray is nowhere close to achieving this. And yet, here he was fielding still another question that for all intents and purposes began with, "Stan, we know you're Swiss and you don't really exist, so tell us about Roger . . ." Wawrinka retweeted a summary of the pregame exchange with Shriver, laughing it off as a "new level" of what's long been par for the course for him. At this year's Australian Open, a spectator wanted to show his support and so between points yelled out, "Let's go, Roger!" The only problem was that it was Wawrinka who was playing, not Federer. "He's not here, he's on Rod Laver!" Wawrinka coolly replied. Rod Laver is the main court of the Australian Open where all the highlight matches take place.

That Wawrinka would end up losing the final at Indian Wells to Federer wasn't a surprise to anyone. Federer had just beaten Wawrinka in the semis of the Australian Open, and of the twenty-three times the two have played, Wawrinka has only won three—all of them on clay. Still, his 4–6, 5–7 loss to Federer at Indian Wells clearly stung. He had taken measure of Roger in Australia and after losing the first two sets stormed back to win the next two before running out of gas in the fifth and final set. And while Federer managed to beat Wawrinka in straight sets, most of the games were closely disputed and came down to a stray return of serve or forehand here or there. At 5–all in the second set Stan lost his serve, which all but sealed his fate. Wawrinka had broken Federer earlier in the match, becoming the only player to break his serve in the entire tournament, but doing so a second time in the match was asking too much. Match point was a microcosm of the entire match. Federer lived between the baseline and the net, pushing his opponent back, robbing him of both time and space. During his press conference after his semifinal win the night

The grass courts of the Desert Springs PBI Tennis Club. (Courtesy of the author)

before, Federer had recalled first hitting with a young Wawrinka many years back and noting how far back behind the baseline he stayed, the strategy of a clay court specialist, which was what, at the time, Federer thought Wawrinka was destined to become. While that hasn't proven to be the case—the obligations of the tour now force players to compete on all surfaces in order to have a

fighting chance for higher rankings and higher seeds—I noted during the final that Federer had turned Wawrinka back into the kid playing ten feet behind the baseline again. A fact that wouldn't have been missed by the astute but on this day helpless Wawrinka. The statistics showed that he hit the ball harder than Federer throughout the match, but Federer hit more winners; Wawrinka's magisterial backhand in particular misfired to the tune of eight unforced errors to only two winners.

After the match, during the on-court ceremony Wawrinka accepted his runner-up trophy choking back tears. He of all people knew how much closer he was, how far he'd come, the string of tough three-set matches prior to the semifinal, staring numerous match points down like a fistful of dwindling firecrackers, while Federer had the unexpected good fortune of getting a walkover in the quarterfinals because the electric and mercurial Nick Kyrgios, who had just routined Djokovic for the second time in two weeks, had to withdraw the day of that match due to illness. Stan stepped to the mic and said that his emotions were the result of being "tired after ten days." Then he said, "I would like to congratulate Roger. He's laughing: he's an asshole." Federer later clarified that he was making faces trying to lighten his friend's mood. It was the only question about Stan that Roger would get.

The men's final pitted Swiss against Swiss. The women's final pitted Russian against Russian: Svetlana Kuznetsova and Elena Vesnina. A flag, however, always only tells part of the story. Federer is from Basel, and his first language is Swiss German; Wawrinka is from Lausanne, and his first language is French. Kuznetsova was born in St. Petersburg (then Leningrad) but is a sketch of Spain: she moved to Barcelona when she was thirteen and speaks Spanish with her coach with native fluency; Vesnina was born in Lviv, Ukraine, studied sports psychology in college, and talks the way she plays: quick, steady, and upbeat.

One of my favorite behind-the-scenes moments of the tournament was when an employee interrupted a triumphant Vesnina's post-match press conference and took the Indian Wells trophy away from her. You see, they only had one actual trophy and they needed it down on the stadium court for Roger Federer's presentation. Vesnina laughed it off with a brightness that came easy to her. You'd think it was the adrenaline of winning, but the truth is that she had been like that for the entire time I was at the tournament. At thirty she has an all-time career high singles ranking of thirteen. The Indian Wells title is only the third singles tournament she's won in fifteen years on the pro tour. Everything clicked for her. Miami might prove to be a different story, but her approach in general set her up for a second spring into her thirties.

I arrived at the stadium court hours before the finals and discovered Vesnina and Kuznetsova sharing the court to practice services with their hitting partners as their coaches looked on. Kuznetsova was peppering the T with serves from the ad court, while Vesnina parted the middle of the deuce court time and again working on her body serve. For a second I thought they were giving away their strategy, but then I recalled that, like Wawrinka and Federer, these two are international teammates in Fed Cup competition. They must have hundreds of hours of shared court time between them if they have any at all. So there they were, together but hardly conscious of the other, sharing the space they would in a little while vie for. Vesnina had endeared herself to the crowd with her solid play and constant post-match expressions of gratitude to the audience. When she played Venus Williams in the quarterfinals she was up against a wall of sound encouraging Venus on. Vesnina won in three hard sets as Venus somehow miraculously fought off some injuries that were clearly hampering her, to extend the match to the maximum. After she won, Vesnina noted what a champion Venus is and thanked the crowd for their great support. This was somewhat of an invention, but it paid off. The crowd embraced Vesnina like one of their own in the semifinal and in the final. *Well played*, I thought. And then, as I watched the Vesnina-Kuznetsova match stretch out over three exciting hours of tennis and people began to wonder when Federer-Wawrinka would start, I began to wonder whether that match

RANKING	MOVE	PLAYER	AGE	POINTS	TOURN PLAYED	POINTS DROPPING
1	–	Andy Murray	29	12,005	18	45
2	–	Novak Djokovic	29	8,915	17	1,000
3	–	Stan Wawrinka	31	5,705	20	10
4	^1	Kei Nishikori	27	4,730	20	600
5	v1	Milos Raonic	26	4,480	20	180
6	^4	Roger Federer	35	4,305	16	0
7	v1	Rafael Nadal	30	4,145	15	10
8	^1	Dominic Thiem	23	3,465	29	90
9	v2	Marin Čilić	28	3,420	21	45
10	v2	Jo-Wilfried Tsonga	31	3,310	18	45
11	–	Gaël Monfils	30	3,190	18	180
12	–	David Goffin	26	2,975	25	360
13	–	Grigor Dimitrov	25	2,960	24	90
14	–	Tomáš Berdych	31	2,790	21	180
15	–	Lucas Pouille	23	2,456	23	90
16	–	Nick Kyrgios	21	2,425	20	360
17	^1	Jack Sock	24	2,375	20	45
18	v1	Roberto Bautista Agut	28	2,190	23	90
19	^4	Pablo Carreño Busta	25	2,025	27	10
20	–	Alexander Zverev	19	1,850	24	25

Official ATP rankings, March 20, 2017. (www.atpworldtour.com)

could live up to this one. I remembered the cliché being batted around in the press, given that all four finalists were over thirty: thirty is the new twenty-one. But as I took in player interviews, players' body language between games, the chess battle of mature point construction that the younger players treat like a coded language, I knew that that's not it at all. Thirty is the new thirty. Someone just needs to say it. What was so great about being twenty-one anyway? As my friend the historian might say: Meh.

TENNIS VANITIES COME TO DUST IN MIAMI

After the Indian Wells finals, I flew from Palm Springs back to New York and the circuit continued on to Miami. Another ninety-six-player-deep Masters 1000 tournament was waiting there for the men, another ninety-six-player-deep Premier Mandatory for the women, the last big hard-court tournament before the seasons of clay and grass. It's hard not to wish that the entire year was like this: the men's and women's tours barnstorming the world together, sharing the spoils and thriving side by side. But malfeasance, logistics, indifference, sloth, and here we are: two tours that flare out into the year only to cross paths like the two strands of a double helix.

The tour will follow the sunshine through the spring and summer until October comes and it resigns itself to life indoors. When I stepped off the plane and out again into Northeast March with its imperfect Northeast weather, I realized how much my sense of tennis is informed by both the weather and distance. Tennis is as much a temperament as a sport to me. And, as much as I had enjoyed being at Indian Wells, I felt a profound happiness in getting back to watching tennis on television in the midst of a changing season instead of a perpetual one.

When I'm at a tournament I tend to find myself a place in an elevated corner and perch there. Many people prefer to be low and close to the court. But I love the geometries of the game and those structures that find their form in the interchange of shots from point to point. That's difficult to see from down on the court. What you see from down close is speed and spin, which is harder to see on television. But what you miss is the geometry, that long game the mind plays as the body's stuck in the short game of swinging and running, swinging and running. Everything has its expense. Proximity is no different. This plays itself out in a large-scale sense of place and fate when it comes to the Miami Open, formerly known as the Sony Ericsson Open, formerly known as the NASDAQ-100 Open, formerly known as the Ericsson Open, and originally named the Lipton International Players Championship.

When, in the summer of 2010, LeBron James announced to a national television audience that he was leaving the Cleveland Cavaliers to sign with the Miami Heat, he famously smiled and said that he was taking his talents to South Beach. The Miami Heat play in AmericanAirlines Arena on Biscayne Boulevard in downtown Miami. South Beach is across the water, twenty minutes or so away depending on the traffic. To arrive there from where the Heat play you'd have to cross Biscayne Bay, either via MacArthur Causeway or, if you don't mind the tolls, Venetian Way. As of the 2010 census the population of Miami-Dade County was 2.5 million; the population of South Beach, 39,186. Unless you work there, nothing compels you to take your talents to South Beach aside from the sun or the rhythm of the night.

But you know what he meant.

By the 1980s, South Beach had already long ago broke bad, but then it broke bad beautifully. *Miami Vice* was as much a play on words back then as "I'm taking my talents to South Beach" would be to anyone now. It's easy for Miami to become, like Barcelona, a beach with a few tall buildings behind it. Beaches don't grow, they shrink. And so, eventually, how can you not feel hemmed in if you think of a city first and foremost that way? Metropolitan Miami spans out for fifty-six square miles, most of which is landlocked. South Beach stands in for Miami Beach which stands in for Miami which stands in for South Beach. The Miami of the mind is a ring of sunshine that glistens and tightens around the temples. It can be a halo or a crown or it can slip down and become a noose. In the end, four years was enough for him, and James found his way back to Cleveland, not University Circle or Buckeye-Shaker—just Cleveland.

The itinerant nature of the circuit is similar. The cities stay still and tennis just misses the mark, setting up shop nearby in more spacious or simply more exclusive environs. A tennis tournament can easily come and go without the city it's named after feeling even the slightest breeze from the tournament passing through. The Miami Open has never been in Miami. It was started at Delray Beach in 1985 by an ex-player named Butch Buchholz and was known then as the Lipton International Player Championships. Buchholz felt there was a void at the start of the tennis calendar, especially given that the Australian Open was played in December back then. There was an opportunity to fill a January-sized gap in the schedule with something big. Perhaps something like a Grand Slam. So he hired Alan Mills, who was a tournament referee at Wimbledon at the time, to work as his head referee. He also hired Ted Tinling as "director of protocol"—Tinling had been the preeminent fashion designer for the women on the women's tour throughout the 1950s, 1960s, and 1970s. Both Mills and Tinling were Englishmen and iconic figures of tennis's recent past. You can see where Buchholz was heading with this: a 128-player draw and both the men's and women's tours playing there concurrently . . . the Lipton wasn't aiming to be another scattered dot on the players' annual itinerary—no, there were bigger plans. It was going to send a shock wave through the circuit by giving the world what it didn't know it was missing: a winter Wimbledon.

That was all fine and good, but a January date wasn't going to happen. The organizers of the Australian Open decided that 1985 would be the last year in which the tournament would take place in December. And so the Lipton settled into a spot in February and was hosted by Rod Laver and his second cousin Ian's Laver's International Tennis Resort, a tennis club and condominium resort complex rolled into one, dropped tidily into a convenient spot in

Delray Beach right between I-95 and Route 1. The prize money that first year was good and brought out stars such as Ivan Lendl, Mats Wilander, Yannick Noah, and a nineteen-year-old Stefan Edberg. Tim Mayotte won the title after the draw collapsed like a house of cards, coming back from two sets down to beat Scott Davis in the final. The women's draw held up better, with the top two seeds meeting in the finals, in which Martina Navratilova beat Chris Evert-Lloyd, the latter having beaten an unseeded fifteen-year-old named Steffi Graf in the semifinals. With four American finalists (Navratilova had become a naturalized citizen) and an intriguing mix of veteran stars and young, up-and-coming talents, and a temperate, vacation-friendly venue staged in the saggy drone of winter, just like at its cousin Indian Wells, things were looking good.

Then, in August of that year, Ian Laver died along with 136 other passengers and crew members in a plane crash in Dallas. The Laver resort would never be the same. The following year, Buchholz moved the Lipton to Boca West, a golf course disguised as a town. The Lipton, still bursting at the seams with a Slam-sized 128-player field, drew in more elite players with Jimmy Connors and Boris Becker entering the fray. Lendl beat Wilander for the men's title, Evert-Lloyd upended Graf in the women's final, but Boca West wasn't the best fit, and so the Lipton would be on the move once again, making it three years of existence and three different venues. This third place would stick, and thirty years later Buchholz's winter Wimbledon, which he sold to IMG in 1999, was still settled in at Key Biscayne's Tennis Center at Crandon Park.

Key Biscayne is an island off the Miami mainland with only one small bridge to serve the flow of traffic, which normally is light, given Key Biscayne's sleepy reputation in comparison to the hot spots that surround it across the water. This contributes to its shifting identity, which, come to think of it, is what many of the places where tennis tournaments settle down have in common. The Miami Open has become, like Indian Wells, a tennis-and-tourism event: three hundred thousand people descend, knowing that the weather will be warm and the game's biggest stars (health permitting) will be playing. However, there's a marked difference between Miami and Indian Wells. The latter holds no pretense to be any place but where it is, eschewing the idea, for instance, that it's the Palm Springs Open. Tennis has enhanced the name Indian Wells, not the other way around. Meanwhile, the Miami Open attracts spectators who want to be in Miami. They want to take their talents to South Beach, not to Key Biscayne. This leads to a daily pilgrimage on and off the island. The bridge swells, traffic stops. Visitors arrive in Miami for the Miami Open and end up stuck in Key Biscayne. For better or for worse, the problem was finally resolved after a long period of disquiet by the Miami Open embracing its transient past, picking up its nets, and once again leaving.

In December 2017, Miami-Dade County agreed to allow IMG to relocate the Miami Open inland to the Hard Rock Stadium in Miami Gardens, home of the Miami Dolphins, which will host the tournament starting in 2019. A few weeks after that announcement, Miami took a page out of the Indian Wells playbook and hired the charismatic retired player James Blake as tournament director.

Winning Indian Wells and Miami back-to-back is known as the Sunshine Double. It's rare and difficult—two consecutive supersized tournaments with the best players on the circuit, one disputed in intense dry heat and the other played immediately after in a haze of thick heat; what's more, if you win Indian Wells you'll end up arriving in Miami with little time to settle in before your first match. Ten players have done it, only two have done it more than once: Novak Djokovic four times (2011, 2014, 2015, 2016—note those three years in a row!) and Roger Federer three times (2005, 2006, and that highly improbable one in 2017).

It already seems long ago now, but I recall people wondering if Federer would even play Miami. Anything after titles at the Australian Open and Indian Wells would be gravy. And the back end of the Sunshine Swing is taxing. In retrospect, this line of thinking was powered by the presumption that Federer would play at least a small part of the clay season. For my part, I thought he'd skip Miami and reserve his body and mind to play only the two bookends of the clay swing, Monte Carlo and the French Open. It never crossed my mind that he would skip clay surfaces entirely. In choosing to do just that, Federer, who had embraced the idea of pacing himself as he went through the year, found himself in a position to do something once and only once in 2017: let it all go, push himself to the limit, knowing that a couple of months of rest were just around the corner. He played fourteen sets: half of them went to tiebreaks. He won three straight rounds where the deciding set was a tiebreak. He had to save two match points in the deciding tiebreak in the quarterfinals against Tomáš Berdych. The scoreline of his semifinal win against Nick Kyrgios, 7–6 (11–9), 6–7 (9–11), 7–6 (7–5), improbably undersells the tension of the match.

Federer and Kyrgios had only met one previous time: in 2015 on clay in a round-of-thirty-two matchup at the Masters 1000 in Madrid. That match also played out in three tiebreakers, the final one in the deciding set won by Kyrgios 14–12. Kyrgios, then ranked thirty-fifth in the world, had already beaten Nadal the year prior, in an early round of the 2014 Wimbledon Championships—not even two weeks past his twentieth birthday, he had already beaten both Federer and Nadal. In Madrid, he blasted twenty aces past Federer and was opportunistic, converting two of the measly three break points he saw during the match. This 2017 match at the Miami Open would mark the third time they had played and the second time in consecutive tournaments. At Indian Wells, Kyrgios remorselessly routined his young friend and counterpart Sascha

Zverev 6–3, 6–4 in the third round before blasting Djokovic off the court in their fourth-round matchup with a display of power tennis rarely seen—performed against the once-in-a-lifetime defensive skills of the great Serbian champion.

Federer was up next in the quarters. The buzz about that match began to build before Kyrgios and Djokovic had even reached the net to shake hands. But that night, Kyrgios drank a shake that didn't agree with him. And the next morning, as fans piled into the stadium at Indian Wells early for what many suspected would be one of the better matches of the year, unofficial word began to circulate around the grounds that Kyrgios was sick and wouldn't be able to play. Federer won by a walkover. The midday sun seemed hotter and more cruel then, as there was little to do or distract from the intense glare and heat. Federer, who had arrived as though the match would go on, came out to address the crowd, thanking them for having come out. Then he entertained the crowd with a video of him, Grigor Dimitrov, and Tommy Haas singing Chicago's "Hard to Say I'm Sorry" accompanied on piano by David Foster. Since Federer, Dimitrov, and Haas all play with one-handed backhands, the group was dubbed the One-Handed Backhand Boys. The crowd was entertained. Federer was once again the winner. If you think moments like that have little to do with what happened one tournament later in the Miami Open semifinal, you would be sorely mistaken.

Kyrgios's path to his first rematch with Federer was a daunting one: after a first-round bye, Damir Džumhur in the second round, the best server on the circuit in the person of Ivo "Doctor Ivo" Karlović in the third round, eighth-seeded David Goffin in the fourth round, and Sascha Zverev again this time in the quarterfinals. Each match was a minefield. Džumhur, twenty-four, was coming into his own. He had beaten Nadal and Berdych the year prior and was fresh off of having survived five match points against future star Hyeon Chung in the first round: 6–4, 6–3 Kyrgios. Playing the punishing six-foot-eleven Karlović is like trying to run in a wind tunnel: you cannot break him, he cannot break you, so you end up alternating winning the games you serve and losing the games he serves until arriving to a tiebreaker at the end of each set: 6–4, 6–7 (4–7), 7–6 (7–2) Kyrgios. Goffin, by contrast, is one of the best returners and steadiest players at the top of the circuit: 7–6 (7–5), 6–3 Kyrgios. This led to Zverev, who in his previous match had dispatched top-seeded Wawrinka with ease. They played three sets, but Kyrgios diced throughout. Zverev, raised from birth to be a tennis player by tennis players, dug out a second-set tiebreaker to force a third set in a match in which an unbothered Kyrgios had taken to hitting running tweeners for winners. The third set proved to be more like the first than the second. A Kyrgios stroll. It took him six match points to put Zverev away, but then he didn't face a single break point over the course of the entire match: 6–4, 6–7 (11–9), 6–3 Kyrgios. Zverev will rack up many wins after this, including against Kyrgios, and at such a young age become a title contender in any tournament that doesn't play five sets. But you watch him and it's hard not to notice that he is a product. He was produced to produce. Kyrgios is a talent dropped from the sky, he's the hero who in this part of the story doesn't want the responsibility. He's not a tennis player for all seasons, one who puts in a dutiful shift wherever whenever for whomever. And yet, when the bell rings and the big moment is upon him, he is a mental blip short of unplayable. The crowds that survived the humidity and the snarling traffic to cross into Key Biscayne were loving seeing this uncharted and barely controlled brilliance first-hand. Until it came up against Roger Federer.

With the match on his racket, serving 5–4 in the third-set tie-breaker against Federer—after having lost a tiebreaker in the first set with nine points and having won a tiebreaker in the second set with nine points—the crowd hated him. They tolerated him at first, when the tennis was exhilarating, the kind of elite-caliber first-strike game-of-chicken tennis that's hard to come by in today's game. There was first hearty applause and then gasps of amazement from the audience as they began to realize that they were watching on the last day of March the best match of the year. And when Federer pulled out a nerve-wracking first set, the audience responded in a way that's unusual when it comes to his matches: nervous relief. He was back to being a world-beater, but was it a temporary return? Was it a dream? Would Key Biscayne be where it all vanished? And would they be the unlucky souls who bought tickets to see it happen live in the flesh? After the first set the answer to all of these questions was no. They had seen better tennis than anyone there had the right to ask for, Federer was out in front, and another final with Nadal waited in the wings. It was the best of both worlds for them on a Friday night.

There's a moment when an audience becomes a crowd. That moment in this Miami Open semifinal matchup happened at some point during the second set when Kyrgios refused to indulge in a dip of form, a lapse in concentration, or a competitive bite, refused to invite wild thoughts that everyone from down courtside to up in the rafters to refreshed in the suites, all of them, wanted Federer to win. Didn't the audience turn into a crowd when they needed to in Federer's last match when he saved two match points against Berdych when they made it clear time and time again as the Czech tried to hold his nerve that they had had enough of him, that they weren't there for him, that he could hit the ball wide or into the net and they would be happy? And didn't Berdych do just that?

There's a moment when an audience becomes a crowd: 5–4 in the second-set tiebreaker, Federer serving from the ad court. In true Miami fashion, it was time to go: the spectacle had been served, Friday night beckoned, and a Federer-Nadal final on American soil beckoned, too. It was time to go. They were both dressed in Nike's vision of hunter green. Kyrgios in the seasonal stock they'd given to their Nike-sponsored players to wear during the Sunshine Swing. Federer, as always, in his personalized line that he alone wears on the tour. Kyrgios, playing to type, separates himself from matching too much with Federer's color scheme by wearing shocks of fluorescent chartreuse in his shorts, socks, and shoes. Federer starts with a kick serve to Kyrgios's two-handed backhand, which, at six foot four and blessed with calm hips and hands, he catches early and on the rise, sending it back down the line with interest on it. Federer is compromised. He takes three lightning-quick steps to his right but still has to lunge for the ball, and here, ironically, does what Kyrgios does so often in this position: he sends back a deep forehand slice to the ad court. Kyrgios, not having left that area, unloads a biting crosscourt backhand that Federer sees before it happens and, having sprinted over to his own ad court, is already there. He whips a heavy crosscourt backhand at Kyrgios. A shot like this isn't designed to end a point or produce an error in the opponent, it instead seeks to stabilize the rally by getting the opponent on the back foot, quite literally, and coaxing a neutral and safe response. It's deep. It clips the baseline. Kyrgios is backpedaling diagonally toward the doubles alley.

What happens next shouldn't under any circumstances happen.

Not only does it disobey the rules of simple tennis physics, it shouldn't be in a player's head to even contemplate precisely, because it's not an option on the physical plane. Kyrgios has backpedaled not out of a need to be defensive but out of a desire to be offensive. Seemingly at the same time the backpedaling stops, the shoulders and hips turn, and the racket's swing path causes the stringbed to clasp and release the ball with furious intent. It speeds over the highest part of the net and finds the line: 5–all. It was a shot that said, *I'm not going anywhere.* The crowd cheered. But then started to roil. Some were no doubt well oiled.

After Kyrgios won the second set, the third became a battle of nerves. Federer's face reflected the seriousness of the situation. Such a warm face, but when troubled the angles make it seem more stern, like a hawk's. Kyrgios, naturally vocal on the court, became more so as the match wore on—berating his decisions, cheering his great play, and, eventually, telling the crowd to shut the fuck up. It was match point for Federer in the third tiebreak, 6–5. Among the effusive cheers for Federer to help and hearten him were also whistles, jeers, and, finally, someone in the crowd calling a ball out in the middle of the final do-or-die point. Game. Set. Match. Federer. Kyrgios responded by shattering his racket on the court, swinging it at the ground like it was a towel on fire that he was trying to put out. Interviewed on the court immediately afterward, Federer thanked the crowd. By that point in the Friday night festivities, Kyrgios had left the court.

There had been a slight air of Jimmy Connors at the 1991 U.S. Open to it, in that the crowd was all in with him and he was riding his luck. Nadal's route to the final had been far less dramatic, although his being bageled by Kohlschreiber to start his third-round match was startling to behold. That said, there was little surprise when Nadal won the next two sets with the minimum amount of fuss. He made his way efficiently to the finals and had less wear on his tires from the Sunshine Swing due to Federer knocking him out of Indian Wells early. Early and rather quickly—that match ran a remorseless sixty-eight minutes. After all of the drama of the closely disputed final in Melbourne, round two in Indian Wells was a disappointment. Now, in Miami, the conditions were different and moving toward Nadal's favor. He was fresher than Federer, had a smoother run through the draw, and was primed to take advantage of the notoriously sluggish court speed of Miami's purple hard-court surface, and his popularity could paper over the fanatical support Federer had been enjoying throughout the tournament and which had clearly overwhelmed both Berdych and Krygios in key moments of their matches. The Miami crowd was in love with Nadal, who addressed the audience post-match in Spanish and, having never won Miami, could be seen as the underdog to cheer for.

Federer beat Nadal for the third time in four months. This time 6–3, 6–4 in a clinical one hour and thirty-five minutes. The final score and the length of the match might lead you to think that things were closer than they were in Indian Wells, but this match was even worse for Nadal. If anything, the conditions in his favor optimized the result for him, but watching the match live was like watching your blender slowly break down a chunk of ice. Nadal faced nine break points in two sets . . . out of nine service games played. And although he saved seven of those break points, he played the match swimming against the current. The Indian Wells matchup had an air of unbelievability to it; even Nadal's face at the end signaled something that was widespread among the viewers: bemusement. This was furthered by the context. Due to their low seeding, the luck of the draw left the two of them on opposite sides of it in the Australian Open, leaving them to meet up in the finals or not at all. At Indian Wells, Nadal was the fifth seed and Federer the ninth: the luck of the draw not only placed them in the same section but resulted in an early-evening match for them. You could possibly look back at Indian Wells, taking all of this in, shrug, and say fair enough. That's basically what Nadal did. But Miami was hard to look at and hard to look away from. Federer had now throttled Nadal in five straight sets: 6–3—in which he won the last five games—and then 6–2, 6–3, 6–3, 6–4. Worse for him, Federer was toying with the tried-and-trusted patterns of point construction that Nadal had relied on in their matchups for years. Worse for us, there was a sense creeping into the fold, a burgeoning lack of astonishment at the result if you watched the matches with an impartial set of eyes and a hardening of January's tender wonder at seeing this rivalry once thought to have run its course now renewed. The two greats were back and on top of the tour again. But I couldn't help starting to wonder whether we're not better off now seeing them apart from one another; whether we'd already reached the point of diminishing returns.

Rafa could worry about that another time. He was without a title but playing better than he had in years. Like Federer, he had his one blip thus far—his Sam Querrey in Acapulco to Federer's Evgeny Donskoy in Dubai. Only one player in the field was keeping up with him. What's more, the red dirt was on the horizon, calling out to him across the ocean. He wouldn't see Roger for months, because even Roger knew Rafa was going to bury everyone he met in the dirt. The result of the final be damned, something at Miami had revealed that change wasn't just on the way, change was already there. Neither player would speak of it, but they must have felt it. Wawrinka came in as the top seed of a Masters 1000 for the first time in his career. He's a wolf who was born to chase, not be chased. He lost in the fourth round. Nishikori was the second seed and lost in the quarters to an unseeded Fabio Fognini, whom Nadal then glided past in the semis. Raonic was the third seed and had to bow out of his second tournament in a row due to injury.

Murray and Djokovic were nowhere to be found.

They were both nursing elbow injuries that had ruled them out of Miami, a tournament neither had missed since 2005. Murray released a public statement on his absence that rang a positive note about the road ahead: "The focus now," he wrote "is on getting ready for the clay season." He didn't know what was coming. But

RANKING	MOVE	PLAYER	AGE	POINTS	TOURN PLAYED	POINTS DROPPING
1	_	Andy Murray	29	11,960	17	0
2	_	Novak Djokovic	29	7,915	16	0
3	_	Stan Wawrinka	32	5,785	20	0
4	^2	Roger Federer	35	5,305	16	0
5	^2	Rafael Nadal	30	4,735	15	0
6	v1	Milos Raonic	26	4,345	20	0
7	v3	Kei Nishikori	27	4,310	20	0
8	^1	Marin Čilić	28	3,385	21	0
9	v1	Dominic Thiem	23	3,385	29	0
10	_	Jo-Wilfried Tsonga	31	3,265	17	0
11	_	Gaël Monfils	30	3,010	17	0
12	^1	Grigor Dimitrov	25	2,880	24	0
13	^1	Tomáš Berdych	31	2,790	21	0
14	v2	David Goffin	26	2,705	25	0
15	^2	Jack Sock	24	2,510	20	150
16	_	Nick Kyrgios	21	2,425	20	0
17	v2	Lucas Pouille	23	2,376	23	0
18	_	Roberto Bautista Agut	28	2,190	23	0
19	_	Pablo Carreño Busta	25	2,025	27	0
20	_	Alexander Zverev	19	2,005	24	0

Official ATP rankings, April 3, 2017. (www.atpworldtour.com)

he'd learn soon enough. We all would. The certainty of the circuit being ruled in 2017 and beyond by Murray and Djokovic was by now anything but clear. Who were the hunted and who were the hunters? They all headed for Europe. It was April, its spring suggestions signaling change in the air. And of the surface. Federer was rampant but had decided to cede the stage, at least for now. From far away, the clay was calling. All the circuit turned toward it slowly like a ship. But no matter how close they came to it, still no one could hear what it was saying. No one could make any sense of it aside from Rafael Nadal Parera.

PART TWO **Spring**

CLAY

The stylish locales of the biggest clay tournaments—Buenos Aires, Rio, Monte Carlo, Barcelona, Madrid, Rome, Paris—belie the true grit at the heart of their tennis. Which is not to say that those cities don't have their rough edges. Of course they do. But tennis and rough edges for the most part tend not to mix. If tennis were a leaf falling onto a stream, it would fall on the placid part, the part in a faraway bend, the picturesque but boring part. An obvious exception to this is the divine comedy that is the U.S. Open, but that's a story of late-summer hard courts that we'll get to later.

Matches on clay courts are a grind. The surface is rooted in a pragmatism made from and infused by the tactile, utilitarian art of ceramics, and it distinguishes itself from other tennis surfaces in its erratic effects. Clay forces a player's body to adapt or fail, a player's mind to obey or die. Shots sponge off the granular surface, slowing down and trampolining back into the air at unlikely angles. Returns that would have been winners on grass and hard courts come ricocheting back to you, sometimes bouncing as high

RANKING	MOVE	PLAYER	AGE	POINTS	TOURN PLAYED	POINTS DROPPING
1	–	Andy Murray	29	11,960	17	360
2	–	Novak Djokovic	29	7,815	16	10
3	–	Stan Wawrinka	32	7,695	20	180
4	–	Roger Federer	35	6,370	16	180
5	–	Rafael Nadal	30	4,955	15	1,000
6	–	Milos Raonic	26	4,490	20	180
7	–	Kei Nishikori	27	3,630	20	0
8	–	Marin Čilić	28	3,370	21	0
9	–	Dominic Thiem	23	3,130	29	0
10	–	Jo-Wilfried Tsonga	31	2,840	17	360
11	–	Gaël Monfils	30	2,770	17	600
12	–	Grigor Dimitrov	25	2,740	24	0
13	–	Tomáš Berdych	31	2,560	21	10
14	–	David Goffin	26	2,420	25	0
15	ʌ1	Nick Kyrgios	21	2,235	20	0
16	v1	Jack Sock	24	2,220	19	0
17	–	Lucas Pouille	23	2,015	23	90
18	–	Roberto Bautista Agut	28	1,900	23	90
19	–	Pablo Carreño Busta	25	1,840	26	0
20	–	Alexander Zverev	19	1,765	24	0

Official ATP rankings, April 10, 2017. (www.atpworldtour.com)

as your shoulders, and players have to slide into their shots. It's hard to stress how difficult it is to adjust to these conditions. Imagine a two-month span of the basketball season in which everyone was forced to play on a thin layer of sand. Suddenly there's a premium on probing, strategic shots over straight-ahead power.

When I was a kid, watching tennis in the wake of the all-court superstars like Chris Evert and Björn Borg, I loved the clay season: it drew my attention to players who weren't often afforded a shot in grass- and hard-court matches. The clay-court specialists: I grew up thinking of them like those poets who had that one great mode in them, spring or death or jazz. They were Spanish, Brazilian, Italian, Austrian, Argentine, and, once in a while, American. Out there on the red earth, they'd sweep up what titles they could while the Pete Samprases of the world bowed out in early rounds, their sure footwork suddenly clumsy. The clay season was a time of difference and entropy, of opportunistic, short-lived dominance.

These days, my daughters wake me up to watch matches across the world. We start early in the morning, before school. They learn about time zones, geography, and the changing surfaces of the tennis year, those seasons unto themselves. For my eldest, who is six now, the greatest mystery about clay isn't how to play on it. Rather, she wonders why everyone calls it red when it's clearly orange. Her younger sister agrees: *It's orange!* As they go about trying to convince me, Frank O'Hara's poem "Why I Am Not a Painter" leaps into my head.

> *But me? One day I am thinking of*
> *a color: orange. I write a line*
> *about orange. Pretty soon it is a*
> *whole page of words, not lines.*
> *Then another page. There should be*
> *so much more, not of orange, of*
> *words, of how terrible orange is*
> *and life. Days go by. It is even in*
> *prose, I am a real poet. My poem*
> *is finished and I haven't mentioned*
> *orange yet.*

Clay gives and takes from your game. It clings to you and—if you let it—weighs you down. For seven weeks, the players were covered in orange dust, match after match, back to front, head to

General view of Court Rainier III during the final of the Rolex Monte-Carlo Masters, April 23, 2017. Roquebrune-Cap-Martin, France. (Photograph by Agence Nice Presse / Icon Sport / Getty Images)

Club Tennis Llafranc. (Courtesy of the author)

toe. The clay bristled underfoot. It wasn't quite summer yet, but the heat had arrived. Clouds were scarce. And the sky was bursting blue. But, as Van Gogh said, there is no blue without yellow and without orange.

The 2017 clay court season. It fills April and May with orange courts, blue backgrounds, a strong yellow sun. I hope you caught some of it. Some of the early months of the tennis year are blue in green, then everything changes. The gravity is different, history is different, hierarchy is an altered state. They are the gas giants of the circuit. Monte Carlo and Roland-Garros a Saturn and Jupiter on the calendar's long string of dates. Rafa Nadal returned to clay looking to consolidate the return to form he'd experienced on the hard courts of Australia and North America. If he was good enough now to play in as many finals as he did on his second-best surface, what would happen when he translated that form onto clay?

He rampaged, winning everything he played on clay but Rome. All roads lead to Paris. He won Monte Carlo for the tenth time, Barcelona for the tenth time, Madrid for the fifth time. Federer— with the rare winter trifecta of the Australian Open, Indian Wells, and Miami in his back pocket—saw what was coming, Nadal grinding everyone down into dust, and decided to skip the clay swing entirely.

Meanwhile, Murray and Djokovic arrived in Monte Carlo still ranked one and two in the world. Yet an object in the rearview mirror was closer than it appeared: Nadal, ranked seventh and rising. He played as though caught in a red mist, obliterating his opponents with controlled fury. Playing Monte Carlo resident Sascha Zverev in Monte Carlo on his twentieth birthday, Nadal gave him the gift of a 6–1, 6–1 beating that had the young German shuffling swiftly off the court at the end of the match as though to hide his tears. It was a message to send back to the locker room: Nadal was here with bad intentions.

Djokovic and Murray, on the other hand, continued with their muddled results, playing as though wading through muddy light. In the quarterfinals, Djokovic faced twelfth-ranked David Goffin of Belgium. Goffin is an excellent all-around player, his slight frame supplemented by his extremely high skill level but not enough as to be a true threat to the few players in the world of Djokovic's caliber. Goffin had not only never defeated Djokovic before, he had won only one set against him in the five matches they'd played against each other. Beat Goffin yet again, and Djokovic would play Nadal in the semifinals. Of the last twelve times Djokovic and Nadal had played, Nadal had won only once; the last three times they had played on clay, Djokovic had not lost. Four months into the 2017 season, already Federer and Nadal had played each other three times, yet neither Djokovic nor Murray had faced either of them even once. It was time to see where everything in this season stood, time for Djokovic to assert himself in this emerging story of the rebirth of two legends and put the hierarchy back in its place. But he lost to Goffin for the first time, 2–6, 6–3, 5–7. The surprise result in that surprise result was Djokovic losing a gut-check final set.

In the third round of Monte Carlo, Murray squandered a first-set lead against the left-handed Albert Ramos Viñolas, one of those thoughtfully skilled throwback players whose game grows two dimensions on the clay. After beating Murray, he continued his good run, defeating fifth-seeded Marin Čilić in the quarterfinals and making it all the way to the finals before facing a 1–6, 3–6 awakening against Nadal. Murray would decide late to accept a wild card to play in Barcelona, to right himself (and maybe to recoup some of his dwindling stash of ranking points). Opportunity smiled on him, or not, as he had the chance to face Ramos Viñolas again; to right himself. Ramos Viñolas continued his scintillating play, hitting wide one moment, deep the next, and tossing in a puckish and perfectly timed drop shot when the occasion called for it—he won the first set 6–2. Not only had Ramos Viñolas now won three straight sets against Murray in little more than a week, he made it look fairly routine. Both of them are curious players in that sense: when Ramos Viñolas is on top of his game and on clay, you'd be forgiven if you thought he was a top-five player; and Murray, despite having carried a twenty-eight-match win streak into the year, has these moments—even in games he ends up winning handily—when his game looks like it fell from the nest of thorns that was cradled high up on an ugly branch of the ugliest tree in the world and hit every ugly branch on the way down to the ground. He adjusts then. The pyrotechnics come. Not the showy cathartic kind: like, say, breaking a racket. No, Murray has this odd type of smoldering explosion where the explosion is definitely happening, you can see it and certainly hear it . . . but it's as though a tarp has been thrown over him. To watch an Andy Murray rant is to watch a passion play by and for the passive-aggressive. Everyone is yelled at and no one is yelled at: he yells and doesn't yell at his coach, his trainer, his wife, his mother, whoever is sitting with them (he doesn't yell at Ivan Lendl, or, if he does, Lendl sits in the box indifferent to it, as though he were the only one to have put on repellent); he yells at himself and his racket and his grip; it seems as though he can reach deep inside himself during some of those difficult moments and yell at his past self, the young pretender to the throne who got pushed around and then beaten to tears on Wimbledon's Centre Court by Federer, the junior who used to lose to Djokovic and Monfils, the twelve-year-old in Barcelona who'd want to ditch practice to watch a match at the Camp Nou. Murray's rage runs deep. It also has proved to be one of the great levelers in the game. It corrects him, brings his barometric pressure to the required place on the scale. He took the next two sets from Ramos Viñolas by force of will, 6–4, 7–6 (7–4). His best tennis? He would have to find that at some other point; now was suddenly about preservation, results. At times, it's the victories that ring the alarm even louder than the defeats. Something was wrong. The next day, Murray would lose the Barcelona semifinal to Dominic Thiem, 2–6, 6–3, 4–6. He would lose in the third round at Madrid to a "lucky loser," a player who had lost in qualifying but made it into the draw as a substitute. Then, in Rome, he'd get obliterated in the second round by Fabio Fognini. At the French Open, he would earn his best results since Doha, arriving to the semifinals and beating del Potro and Nishikori along the way before losing in five sets to Stan Wawrinka. And there's certainly no shame to losing at Roland-Garros to Wawrinka, who won the title on that very same court in 2015 and has as many Grand Slam titles as Murray. But it would be a stretch to say that he looked particularly good in any of those matches, some of which it almost seemed he won on the strength of reputation. Even against Wawrinka, having scratched out a two-set-to-one lead, when forced to a fifth set he faded quickly, looking off the pace and incapable of generating any power at all. His game seemed stripped of its vitality.

For those looking for the 2016 vintage of Andy Murray in 2017 or for the 2017 version to reach even greater heights, it was time instead to lower expectations. Though he began the year in good form in Doha, cracks after that had started to appear and were widening. He lost early at the Australian Open, early at Indian Wells, early at Monte Carlo, early at Madrid, and early at Rome. And by the time the dust cleared on the clay season he was still the number-one-ranked player in the world. Such is the power of the past.

Did he run himself into the ground the year prior in search of the year-end top ranking? Or were these the inevitable injuries of a player now in his thirties? If, at the start of 2017, someone were to tell you that Djokovic would lose in the second round of the Australian Open and in the quarterfinals of the French, it would have been difficult to imagine that Murray wouldn't end up with either of those titles. But here he was, suddenly and strangely eclipsed. Eclipsed and, like Djokovic, hardly missed. You couldn't quantify it, but you could sense it. With the return to champion-ship form of first Federer and now Nadal, tennis brimmed with a joy and wonder and spectacle that it hadn't enjoyed in some time. What would Murray do to get back into the thick of things? It was the ninth of June. He would play in only two more tourna-ments the rest of the year.

THE GHOST IN THE DIRT

The clay season is a ghost story. It always has been. There's a ghost in the red dirt. He ran hotels for a living and, oddly enough given how things have turned out in tennis, he was Swiss. You have never heard of him. And, no judgments, but he was a bit of a hustler. His tremendous ambition coupled with his creative bookkeeping forced him into bankruptcy twice. His name was Georges Henri Gougoltz. He spent the last decades of his life as a hotel propri-etor by name but in reality owing important men a considerable amount of money. After they took his hotel from him, he was obliged to run that gold mine he had developed from the private castle it once was as though nothing had changed—a figurehead to smile at and arrange things for the ever rising number of foreign elites who wintered there seeking out the sun, their social peers, and the increasingly famous red clay courts of the Hôtel Beau-Site in Cannes, France.

When I tell you that he killed himself on a January morning in 1903 by shooting himself in the head not once and not twice but three times—you probably won't believe that he killed him-self. And you probably shouldn't.

We'll never know exactly what happened to him, but when, in 2017, Nadal lifted La Coupe des Mousquetaires ebulliently over his head for a tenth year, standing proudly on a makeshift podium

The back of a dinner menu at the Hôtel Beau-Site, 1880. This gives an early idea of how Gougoltz thought to promote the hotel: prominently placed on a hill surrounded by other grand estates. Note the absence of tennis courts in this promotion, along with the prominence of Gougoltz himself. (Property of the author)

at the center of that rectangle of brick-red in the middle of Roland-Garros's show court, Gougoltz's crushed-ceramic sand courts—the ones that once graced the foot of the hill of the Beau-Site just past the lush and sloped sculptured courtyard, like a mirage of politely placed tonnage of light-red dust at the edge of a politely placed jungle of imported greenery—were with him there, inhuman and yet veritably part of him, a 150-year-old first idea.

Myth, legend, and truth: they work on their own time and make their own order—they're brilliant and terrible. This story has never been and will always be about a man's suicide in the face of crushing financial debt: we'll get to that. And this story has never been and will always be about Rafael Nadal's run as the master of clay-court tennis. The two collided, unwittingly, on a warm Sunday afternoon in early June in Paris, 2017, when Nadal once again won the French Open in front of a crowd packed into Court

Philippe Chatrier. It was his tenth title there, his tenth time turning the orange dust into a celebratory scene for the rarest of synergy between player and surface, a gift that at times has seemed as sacred as a covenant, a strange bond between him and the ground. To celebrate the achievement, the powers that be at the French Open had ready a montage of Nadal playing a point in which, stroke by stroke, he aged a year and the tournament advanced a year, so that the final point was match point of the 2017 men's final: the past catching up with the present, present alive in the past.

Sports strain to stress to us that we are watching history, and the Fédération Française de Tennis didn't want to let slip the opportunity to make that literal. And yet, the spectacle of Nadal's achievement began 150 years ago from that moment. In the age of history and myth, sometime before the first orangish grains of sand were pulverized into life and in turn gave life to the game of tennis on clay. Before Nadal or Kuerten or Muster or Noah or Evert or Borg, in the beginning there was myth, with all of its typical daydreams of heroes and genius. And before that, in the beginning of that beginning, there was the empty Château Court, looking down on a grass field from its slight hill on the west end of Cannes, and, looking up at it, with dreams of grandeur in his eyes, was a hotelier from Switzerland who would live and then die, tragically and horrifically, with the clay. Rafa Nadal's tenth French Open title began 150 years ago on that day when, in 1867, Bruno Court sold his château to Gougoltz.

It turns out that everything Gougoltz had done in Cannes was synchronized with the birth and rise of tennis. He just hadn't known it. He was timed to tennis. But France had yet to catch the sporting fever that the English were already fully in the grip of. Despite tennis being a selling point for hotels and villas advertising in the travel books flying off the presses in England in the late 1870s, *Le Courrier de Cannes et de la Provence* wouldn't even mention tennis until

November 1883. It would already be a staple of the *vie mondaine* of the winter residents by then and, as though catching up on lost time, the *Courrier* inserted the activity into its "Society Life" section of the front page: "Mornings are filled with horseback riding and lawn tennis is at the same time the most fashionable sport around and a solitary exercise." But before then, as 1880 quickly approached, Gougoltz could take solace in the fact that he was at the cusp of something, just as he had been barely a decade earlier when he arrived in Cannes and bought Bruno Court's château on the hill. And look at how well that had gone for him. It was fate. Besides, hadn't the Englishman Walter Clopton Wingfield cobbled together lawn tennis the same year, not very long after he had expanded the Beau-Site? Wasn't it a sign? All of that land, the sumptuous gardens, the hill from which guests descend to the pageantry of the lawn. It had always felt somewhat incomplete, its potential slightly unrealized. The Hôtel Gray d'Albion had taken to advertising both that the Prince and Princess of Wales had visited and that the ground contained lawn tennis courts—"Every modern comfort," the advertisement beamed at the end. How do you top a hotel with both tennis courts and a royal pedigree? First, he would have to start with the tennis courts. A few months later, in May 1880, the following appeared in *Bradshaw's Continental Railway, Steam Transit, and General Guide, for Travellers Through Europe*:

HOTEL BEAU SITE.

SITUATED on the West end of Cannes, adjoining Lord Brougham's property, the finest part of the town. Newly enlarged 200 rooms: 20 private Sitting-rooms: Reading, Smoking, and English Billiard rooms. Bath Rooms. Lift. Sheltered situation commanding an unequalled view of the Sea, the St. Marguerite Islands, and the Esterel Mountains. Large beautiful gardens and promenades belonging to the estate, with extensive Croquet Ground and Lawn Tennis. Arrangements made for the season for families. Charges moderate. Omnibuses at the Station. Opened 1st October.

GEORGES GOUGOLTZ, Proprietor.

By 1880 Gougoltz knew that tennis was what he had been missing. He also knew then that he had to make up for lost time. And so, this is when the story began.

The year was 1880 and the biggest stars of the tennis world, the Renshaw brothers, Englishmen born into comfort, were frequenters of the Beau-Site during the winter months. They would train there and also give lessons to other guests in what one local paper referred to as *le jeu à la mode*, the fashionable game. Tennis on the lawn of the Beau-Site played out like theater, given the pavilion at the base of the hotel that looked down onto the courts and the shaded sitting areas in the spectacular gardens surrounding them. Unlike Monaco, it wasn't the rush of gambling, though the spectacle and excitement were similar and more earnest. But the heavy use of the turf along with the rather un-English climate put a strain on the surface that threatened to leave it not only unplayable but also unsightly.

The Renshaw brothers, as the story goes, then came up with an ingenious plan: they ordered as much clay ceramics and brick as they could from nearby Vallauris, a small town with a rich tradition in pottery; after having the material pulverized, they had the fine sand—with its peculiar hints of burnt sienna, orange, and cinnamon—cover the turf; and, voilà, the surface proved a success. It took hold throughout the region. To add to the legend, the Renshaws returned home to England stronger than ever. Both had lost at Wimbledon in 1880, but in 1881 Ernest won Dublin (back then a highly prestigious tournament) and William won Wimbledon for the first time in his career and for the following five years after. Overall, he'd win seven Wimbledon titles over nine years, those seven titles being a record he'd hold (eventually along with Pete Sampras) until Federer won his eighth title in 2017. He faced Ernest in the final three of those years. Ernest won Wimbledon in 1888 and the Irish Championship in singles on four separate occasions. Together they won five Wimbledon doubles titles.

At some point the story settled on the brothers, the Beau-Site, and the date of either 1880 or 1881 when the Renshaws convinced the owner of the Beau-Site to let them redesign the court in order to protect the lawn from the wear and tear that came with their constant play. Grass courts suffer from play in a way that croquet lawns never did, and upkeep so that they remain both playable and pleasant on the eyes is costly and time-intensive. As well as the money and style that tennis potentially brought in to a hotel, it brought with it substantial and constant expense for upkeep. The owner of the Beau-Site at this point was, of course, none other than Gougoltz. But, aside from a brief mention in the second edition of Heiner Gillmeister's *Tennis: A Cultural History*, Gougoltz practically doesn't exist. This despite the fact that he was the owner, developer, and manager of the hotel where the clay game as we know it now began. He would have been at this time up to his neck in his third major renovation of the hotel, the grand dining room, and a year removed from the addition of the western pavilion. Up until this moment he had managed to stay ahead of financial disputes and threats of litigation. But more charges of financial impropriety and failure to repay debts began to circle around him.

Imagine, then, his great luck when the two biggest stars in England's most popular game not only happened to be wintering at the Beau-Site but also felt an unprecedented, never-duplicated, and never-spoken-of inspiration to design tennis courts, and approached the beleaguered Swiss entrepreneur with an offer not only to make innovative and eye-catching tennis courts but also to do so out of their own pocket.

Yet, the Renshaws were such a known commodity in their day that they had a tennis shoe named after them: the "Renshaw lawn-tennis shoe" (essentially an oxford with a rubber sole) made by Hickson and Sons and advertised in the mid-1880s in magazines such as *Pastime*. Images of the Renshaw twins were iconic. They were the first superstars of tennis. And yet there doesn't exist a single record anywhere of the Renshaws' involvement with the Beau-Site courts. The local papers would run a story of someone sneezing on someone else if they were the right people. Reports of cockfighting and gardeners' affairs made the papers. And yet they have nothing about the Renshaws' invention, much less a sighting of them at the Beau-Site at any time before 1885. Although Ernest died young, William spent his retired life around tennis players and enthusiasts during the legendary years of the Beau-Site tennis courts, and yet William Renshaw said nothing of them. It appears, rather surprisingly, that no one asked him.

So where are we, now? A famous clay court (the first of its quality and kind), famous twin tennis players during the rise of print media, and the idea of modern celebrity as we know it today. And yet there's absolutely nothing on record about the Renshaws' doing anything but playing on these courts years after they were made. The courts were so famous for their clay that a historical record was being kept as early as 1900, when Georges Gougoltz was still alive. A tennis enthusiast from London named John Simpson wintered at Beau-Site from 1879 on. He remembered William Renshaw first coming to Cannes in 1886 and beating everyone he played with ease.

Everyone, in this case, included Dr. James Dwight, one of the pioneers of lawn tennis in America—he is widely considered to have played the first game of tennis in America with Dick Sears—and, in 1881, was one of the founders of the U.S. National Lawn Tennis Association. Renshaw demolished Dwight. Nevertheless, the social imprint of the two players had come to be such that, although the match itself didn't make the news, their departure

A pictorial account of a Wimbledon match between the Renshaw brothers in the 1880s. (Photograph by Bob Thomas / Popperfoto / Getty Images)

1880. WILLIAM RENSHAW AND ERNEST RENSHAW

William and Ernest Renshaw of England, the first superstars of tennis, and considered by most accounts the architects of the French red clay court. This is more than likely a false claim. (Photograph from Hulton Archive / Getty Images) did: "Messrs. Dwight and Renshaw, the famous champions of 'Lawn-Tennis' have just left Cannes where they lived at the Beau-Site," the *Courrier* dutifully reported. By this point Georges Gougoltz was still listed as the proprietor of the Beau-Site, but he was utterly, and rather publicly, bankrupt. He owed the important men of town an unfathomable amount of money. He tried to use his bankruptcy to clear himself of having to pay back his debts, just as the hotel was experiencing its boom. An angry lender took him, once again, to court. His partners were so pleased now with the great draw that the Beau-Site had become that they tried to pay him off and let Gougoltz continue doing what he did best. The clientele came from all parts now, because the Cannes of fishermen had become the Cannes of the fashionable, and tennis had them crazed—word spread of a court like none other among the old money, new money, social climbers, schemers, and romantic tennis lovers: the magnificent Hôtel Beau-Site.

The sportswriter Arthur Wallis Meyers spent thirty years covering tennis for *The Daily Telegraph* and *The Field*. (He also competed in the French Open, U.S. Open, and Wimbledon in his forties—those were other times.) In his book *The Complete Lawn Tennis Player*, he recollected that the courts of the Beau-Site were "a surface second to none in France." And that they were "made of a particularly fine and adiactinic sand, indigenous to the district, which rolls out to perfection, especially after a light shower. They receive, as all good courts should, careful and minute attention at the hands of experienced gardeners who, with their brooms, hose and rollers, are always to be found in early attendance." Who would hire these gardeners? Who would train them in the nuances of tending for a clay court? Who would set their schedules to coincide with court times? Meyers wouldn't ask these things. No one seemed to. The general attitude to luxury was, and in many ways still is, that what went into it should remain invisible, and this was

The clay courts of the Beau-Site were so famous that they became the subject of the postcard themselves. The hotel becomes an afterthought to the tennis, receding to the backdrop and obscured by the canopies of trees. (Photographer unknown; property of the author)

perhaps best coined by an early editorial in the *Courrier* on Gougoltz and the Beau-Site: "We do not wish, of course, to enter into a description of luxury, which would make it less lovely. Suffice it to say that the thing could not be more perfect."

There came an era when Gougoltz's three clay courts were the epicenter of tennis on the Continent, providing the bedrock for the connection with the clay game that it enjoys to this day. Gougoltz's son and his nephew Jean, who would go on to become a world-famous cyclist, were often ball boys for matches where the players ranged from King Gustav V of Sweden to France's Suzanne

A postcard from the Beau-Site, 1901. The three clay courts in the foreground of the hotel. (Property of the author)

The front of a New Year's Day menu at the Hôtel Beau-Site. (Property of the author)

Lenglen, in those days already a living legend of the game. Gougoltz, however, reaped little in the way of benefit from this: he had been forced to declare bankruptcy in 1884 and again in 1902.

Meanwhile, the tennis there continued to occupy the public imagination. The courts would be the site for the greatest tennis painting of them all, John Lavery's 1929 oil-on-canvas *Tennis Under the Orange Trees, Cannes*. It depicts a doubles match on the Beau-Site. The server is in a flowing and sporty white dress, mid-motion, at the height of her toss, racket back, her feet in the platform stance, somewhat like the trophy position. In the purple-shadowed foreground, a canopy of orange trees in *repoussoir*, leading the viewer's eye from the trees to the court and pushing the court forward into the trees so that they are two spaces at once; so much so that the ball is unsighted due to the trees and it looks like the server is about to strike one of the oranges off its branch. The returner, like the server, is in white. Their partners, both at the net, are in collaborating orange and red sweaters. Behind them, the vagueness of the background suggests maybe more garden, perhaps the sea, an uncertain sky, an undefined world.

And yet, by the time of Lavery's painting the hotel's courts had settled into their late fate as more of a curiosity of the first phase of the French Riviera. The Beau-Site courts were on borrowed time. The First World War had changed the landscape. And there was the tennis club at the Cannes Carlton that left the casual affairs of Beau-Site in its large shadow. Suzanne Lenglen and Helen Wills would play their historic match there.

Cannes wasn't destined to be the center of tennis forever. Places like the Beau-Site were for idle play, small niche tournaments, handicapping and casual bets between friends. Tennis and Cannes both continued to grow but they grew apart. As early as 1887, Renshaw and Dwight took their act from Cannes to Nice, where

John Lavery, *Tennis Under the Orange Trees, Cannes*, 1929, oil on canvas. (Private collection; reproduced from *Court on Canvas: Tennis in Art*)

it was more permissible to let your competitive juices flow and truly strike a ball with anger. Tennis there was, in Meyers's words, "naturally of a more serious character than it is in Cannes . . . Competitors feel, as it were, that they have the eyes of the outside world upon them, whereas at the Beau Site the warriors are occasionally crying a halt to tension." And then later, the greatest competition in the region settled in where it was always destined to be and remains to this day, with the high rollers in Monaco, a complex of pristine red clay courts caressed by a mountainside and the sea—the first of three Masters 1000 tournaments on the clay swing of the circuit.

Monaco has long since moved on from and eclipsed Cannes. It has its own tennis history and its stories now. Like how, in 2014, two Swiss men faced each other in the final there, making it the first time a Swiss would lift the trophy. Wawrinka emerged from the brink of death in the second set and strolled in the third to take the title from Federer. It was the fourth time Federer had lost the Monaco final—earlier in his career he lost three years in a row to Nadal. The Swiss legacy on clay has been one of many more losses than wins, and some of them quite brutal. Still, for my money Federer is the second-best player I've ever seen on the surface. But he doesn't have much to show for his performance there aside from the art of it and a few cherished titles. Although, even without them we'd speak of him on the clay. Because of both him and Wawrinka, with one French Open title each, we could say we owe the Swiss their due. Today, there are no tournaments in nearby Cannes to speak of. Certainly not in this way. And no one speaks of the Swiss who started it all, Georges Henri Gougoltz. The ghost in the dirt.

THE BALLAD OF DAVID GOFFIN

By the end of the clay swing David Goffin had every reason to believe that he was cursed. Not a may-the-world-immediately-come-crashing-down-on-your-head kind of curse but a Sisyphean curse, a long-game curse. The kind of curse you don't realize has been put on you until it finally descends to tell you straight to your face that, yes, you've been cursed. He began 2017 ranked eleventh in the world, as high as he'd ever been. His early-season results were encouraging: he made it to the quarterfinals of the Australian Open before losing in straight sets to Dimitrov, and he made the finals of the next tournament he played, the Sofia Open in early February, where he lost to local hero Dimitrov once again.

Fair enough. But when he lost again in the finals of the next tournament he played, 4–6, 6–4, 1–6, to France's Jo-Wilfried Tsonga in Rotterdam just one week later, I began to wonder when exactly was the last time I remembered David Goffin actually winning a tournament.

By the time he'd arrived in Monte Carlo in mid-April, he'd been a top-twenty player for two years and was surging into the top ten. A tennis player can ride a string of results over the course of a year or a part of a year and end up with an inflated ranking, but a player has to defend the points won the prior year or they're lost: if a player makes a Grand Slam semifinal one year and follows that up by getting eliminated in the first round of the same Grand Slam tournament the following year, that player can kiss 1,190 ranking points goodbye. Coming into Monte Carlo in 2017, Goffin's consistency over the past few years left it clear that he was as good as his ranking said he was, maybe even better.

Add to that the admittedly subjective category of the eye test, which he passes with flying colors. He's a technician with an attractive game that's burdened by few weaknesses aside from a rather noticeable lack of heft. Perhaps that's what's slowed him down thus far this year against Tsonga in the final in Rotterdam and against Dimitrov in the final in Sofia, and in 2016 against Kyrgios in Tokyo and in 2015 against Thiem at the Swiss Open in Gstaad and Nicolas Mahut in that same year at the Rosmalen Grass Court Championships in 's-Hertogenbosch and at the end of 2014 against Federer in Basel. Those are all large gentlemen, Federer at six foot one being the runt of the group; two of the finalists—Federer and Dimitrov—were playing at home; by the end of the clay season Kyrgios and Thiem will both have beaten Djokovic this year and they've both beaten Federer; and playing Mahut on the grass is going to be a handful for even the very best players on the circuit. So mitigating circumstances abound. Nevertheless, Goffin began his first-round match on the clay courts of the 2017 Rolex Monte-Carlo Masters without a single title to his name since winning a 250 indoor hard-court title—the Moselle Open in Metz, France—all the way back in September 2014, when he was the forty-sixth-ranked player in the world.

Spring had barely arrived in 2017, and Goffin had already seen two chances on hard court to break his dry spell come and go. Now came the clay, and he was a good clay player. In fact, his first-ever title was on clay, although it was a smaller tournament staged in the middle of the hard-court swing and none of the big players were there. Monte Carlo is an entirely different proposition. It's not a mandatory Masters tournament like the others on the calendar, but it is the first major clay date on the calendar. It's the best place to signal to others on the tour your intent for the clay season. After all, Rafa had done so by winning it nine times. Federer has tried repeatedly and failed to ever win it. Goffin knew he'd have his hands full, but this was the year of his great push. He knew it.

What he didn't know was that he'd get utterly screwed.

The quintessential offensive baseline player, he is the personification of precision. His forehand is contemporary, he holds his racket so that when he makes contact with the ball his palm is facing upward toward the sky, and produces spin easily. It has good pop to it, enough to push an opponent around the court when needed, although it's lacking some power, that power having been exchanged at some point in his formation for uncanny, rhythmic accuracy. The less that's said about his backhand, the better—such things shouldn't be spoken of or written about, as words will struggle to do it justice. He swings it as though he's been chosen out of thousands to hit that one gong at the end of a live performance of Queen's "Bohemian Rhapsody" and takes to it calmly and on time with two hands gripping the stick—it is imperious, so much so that it verges on ridiculous. Tennis is a game centered on errors, nothing about it is perfect, and yet when David Goffin strikes a backhand, even when he makes an error with it, it is perfect.

His serve is good enough, varied enough to keep him out of trouble more often than not, and he is an elite returner, one of the top ten in the men's game. He is the paradigm of the well-balanced player, his strengths and lesser strengths (he doesn't really have weaknesses) in constant conversation and finding a state of equilibrium from shot to shot, point to point, game to game, set to set, match to match. The bedrock under all of this is how he handles pressure. The ATP keeps track of a statistic it calls an Under Pressure Rating, which combines how a player deals with moments when a match is most ready to tilt one way or the other— percentage of break points converted, percentage of break points saved, percentage of tiebreaks won, percentage of deciding breaks won. In 2017, he would finish eighth. He is slight, has small, clear eyes and a tall forehead on top of which is a healthy-looking flop of champagne-blond hair that he wears in a polite but messy, minimum-fuss haircut that both mother and son would agree to the latter getting at the salon. At five-foot-eleven he is neither short nor tall, but he weighs around 150 pounds, which makes him seem smallish, and the light canvas of stubble he tends to leave on his face doesn't hide the fact that, although he'll turn twenty-seven just after the 2017 season is over, he looks barely old enough to rent a car.

He was born in Rocourt, Belgium, and his name is pronounced something like "Go-fah." His father was his first coach and still coaches back in Belgium. His native country has produced all-time great players on the WTA tour—champions such as Justine Henin and Kim Clijsters, both having been recently elected to the International Tennis Hall of Fame—as well as a number of top-twenty-ranked women such as Kirsten Flipkens, Elise Mertens, and Yanina Wickmayer. Goffin, on the other hand, is the best male player in Belgium by a country mile and has been for some time. The only other Belgian man in the top one hundred is fifty-first-ranked Steve Darcis, a thirty-three-year-old with a one-handed backhand who has risen and dipped between the fifties and one-fifties in the rankings for the past ten years. And here they were now, as they had been in the quarterfinals in Bulgaria, across the net from each other on Monte Carlo's first day of matches. As was the case in Bulgaria, Goffin handled Darcis with ease: this time 6–2, 6–1. And in the second round he weathered the body blows of the powerful Almagro in the first set before speeding past him in the second with another 6–1. Next up was another big hitter with a thunderous one-handed backhand and powerful serve but a better overall package—the ninth-ranked Dominic Thiem of Austria, who's a fixture in the top ten but whom Goffin had proved in the past to have the measure of—he'd defeated him in the round of sixteen of this year's Australian Open, as he had the year before as well. Of the eight matches they had played thus far, Goffin had won five. Thiem is a dangerous, bruising opponent, but Goffin couldn't help but feel comfortable and ended up winning in three sets.

Then came the win over Djokovic in the quarterfinals.

Goffin had failed in thirteen prior attempts to beat a top-three player on the tour. It was as though he needed to bypass the unlucky number to break free of the jinx. Little did he know.

Djokovic had spent the week up to his neck in tight matches. He had to escape two tough three-set matches in the prior rounds.

Despite a string of subpar results throughout the 2017 season up to this point, Djokovic played quite well in this match. But Goffin tapped into a vein he'd been hiding from the world: he played the deciding set with the vigor of a champion. He was playing with the extra gear and the extra reserves at the money end of the fight. At 4–all in the third with Goffin serving, 30–30, they played a thirty-seven-second, twenty-six-shot rally. It was gut-check time, and Djokovic's amazing defenses are designed in part to cause the opponent to flinch during just these moments. What else is there to do when your best shot, one you thought would win you the point, comes right back at you? But Goffin wouldn't blink. The Belgian dictated the point from start to finish, answering every shot from the Serb with something extra, pulling him one way and then another around the court until a clear lane down the line opened up and Goffin stepped back into the doubles alley of the ad court to unleash an unreachable inside-in forehand down the line. He pumped his fist, blew into his cupped right hand to cool it down, then calmly walked across the baseline to serve for the game at 40–30. No hysterics. No surprise. He was where he wanted to be and where he should be.

When Djokovic's last shot fell weakly into the net, his fore-hand once again overpowered by a blistering backhand from the Belgian, Goffin dropped his racket, raised his arms victoriously, and looked up into the sky. The sun had been swallowed up by the more mischievous side of spring—the scenic Mediterranean backdrop of Monaco's main court was suddenly more ominous: dark clouds and muddy winds circled through the stadium. I watched on a laptop at a desk in a room in an inn in Wooster, Ohio, where I was for work. At some point that afternoon I would give a talk, but made sure to keep the first half of my day clear. I remember feeling more surprised about the weather than the result. Goffin had been building toward this win for a year. But the Monaco on my monitor suddenly seemed as blustery as the Ohio outside my window. Goffin had Nadal next. With Federer wrapped up in cotton until the summer, they were the two hottest players on the tour. Such was random chance, the luck of the draw, etc., that they'd never played each other on the circuit before. Nadal had nine of these titles already. But no one on the circuit had won more matches in 2017 than Goffin's twenty-three. He had every reason to feel battle-tested and ready, to like his chances on the dirt against the King of Clay.

He was doomed.

As soon as Nadal finished off Goffin in straight sets in the semifinal 6–3, 6–1, a shock wave of boos blasted down on the court from the stands.

Nadal made his way to the net with his gaze downward and went to shake hands with Goffin, who was already waiting there for him like a person with somewhere else to be. You never know what types of platitudes, intimacies, or empty words are shared at the net after a match, but none were shared here. Nadal, as is custom, shook the chair umpire's hand. Goffin walked by Cédric Mourier like he wasn't there, packed as quickly as he could, lugged his tennis bag over his shoulder, and started to make his way off the court. Cheers followed him. He turned to wave. And then he was gone. He'd won four games, but the crowd had come to favor him reverently for the final twelve games of the match. At his post-match press conference Nadal would say that there were no boos at the end of the match. During the incident, yes; but not at the end of the match. This is untrue, but Nadal is a master of his mindset. The crowd may not have been booing Rafa, but they were booing. Loudly. They spent the last hour finding any excuse to boo. They were booing that the makings of a great match had been taken from them. But most of all, they were booing at how terrible the chair umpire was. And make no mistake about it, the moment

Cédric Mourier poured himself down from his elevated little chair in the shade in the middle of the first set, no good was going to come of it for anyone.

It took five rounds of tennis on the clay over five days for the curse to come out to play. This is how it works: you beat the obstacles in your way, clear them from your line of sight (how one of those obstacles invariably ends up being a worse version of yourself), and you discover yourself in a moment you think will define you, not the peak of your life but a higher level seen in the distance for some time now—this is when the fates come for you, the curse clears its throat and says your name, the ghost in the dirt stirs.

Ahead 3–2 in the first set, Goffin already with a break and looking to consolidate it with a hold: after four deuces, it's advantage Goffin, one point from 4–2. He's been all over Nadal, carrying over his considerable momentum from the Thiem and Djokovic matches. Nadal wasn't supposed to look like this, not on clay. Goffin was taking the initiative every moment he could, pulling Nadal from corner to corner with a smart combination of whipping topspin forehands and penetrative backhands that time and again found the deepest corners of the court.

This wasn't supposed to be part of Rafa's story.

He'd started his clay season by bageling England's Kyle Edmund in the first set before losing 5–7 in the second and turning the tables without much ado in the third, 6–3. But after the match Nadal was furious. Edmund shouldn't have been any kind of a threat to him on clay, and if he wanted to get to the French Open in maximum physical condition, then he couldn't go losing long sets in the early rounds of Monte Carlo, Barcelona, Madrid, or Rome to players he should be throttling into submission from the get-go. Nadal hit the ground running against Edmund, winning the first set 6–0. But the second set had been a sign of something that disgusted him: relaxation. It was a beautiful afternoon on the coast but, unsatisfied with his performance, Nadal put in some extra practice. The next day he played Sascha Zverev, who lives in Monaco and was celebrating his twentieth birthday. From the first moments of warm-ups Nadal looked like he was trying to set fire to anything he laid his eyes on with his glare alone. I hit pause, got up, and made some popcorn. When I came back, I got a pillow and propped my feet up. The 6–1, 6–1 beating he put on Zverev was utterly brutal, cruel and yet somehow bloodless, like only Nadal can do: a hot knife cutting through butter not because it has to but because that's what's there. Zverev couldn't get off the court quickly enough. It was his birthday. Rafa didn't care. There'd be better days ahead for him. After a routine 6–4, 6–4 win against the Argentine Diego Schwartzman, it was time not for Djokovic but for Goffin.

Ahead 3–2 in the first, Goffin already with a break and looking to consolidate it with a hold: after four deuces, it's advantage Goffin, one point from 4–2. It's a quick point: Nadal hits a running forehand six inches clear of Goffin's baseline. The line judge calls "Out," forcefully, clearly. The audience applauds. Nadal walks toward the ball kid who has the towel to dry himself off and reset to serve down 2–4. Goffin goes to do the same.

There's a moment when you realize something's about to happen. When the air changes slightly or the color of the sky suddenly warps. I had turned to do something while the players prepared for the next game, but I suddenly realized something was missing from the point they'd just played, when Nadal's shot had clearly—beyond clearly—landed half a foot out and the line judge called "Out." I hadn't heard, *Game: Goffin. Goffin leads four games to two.*

Why was Mourier walking toward some random mark in the

dirt? Why had Mourier come down from his chair in the first place?

Remember that players are granted three challenges per set and if a challenge is deemed correct the player isn't charged for having used it. The process is quick, efficient, and—despite the occasional bemused reaction from a player—definitive. Hawk-Eye has unquestionably changed tennis for the better.

Clay-court tournaments do not use Hawk-Eye. The rationale is that, unlike grass and hard courts, the surface of a clay court is in constant motion, brushed this way and that by the players' feet, the vagaries of the wind, and other such stuff, and therefore, between when a ball is hit and when it lands on the dirt, the surface may have shifted not once or twice but countless times. The idea of a fixed mark, then, would be an unreliable one. Clay is another variable in the equation. So for clay tournaments and only clay tournaments tennis takes us back in time: the chair umpires still come down from their chairs to inspect marks as in the old days when there's a dispute.

No one had disputed that Nadal's shot was out, just as no one disputed that the sun was in the sky. It was out, tennis like life was moving on to whatever the next chapter on this Saturday was supposed to be. But Cédric Mourier saw something. A common adage in sports is that the better the umpire or referee, the less he or she is seen. If you watch tennis at all, you may not know him by name, but you will recognize Cédric Mourier. Not by any remarkable power of charisma or distinguishable physical trait. You recognize him by his constant and utterly perplexing compulsion to involve himself in a tennis match. It's one thing not to see well or to invent things, but Mourier does both under the trained eyes of players and the gaze of both public and televised audiences time and time again. He has spent years to the exasperation of many seeing things no one else has seen. Once, in

Madrid in 2013, he called a ball in that was close to a foot wide. It was a serve that bounced right in front of his chair. Nadal, who was the receiver, was cruising in the match, but was utterly perplexed and protested anyway, as one would and should when you're suddenly left to wonder what the rules of the sport are. Once, in 2008, Mourier made such a hash of a match between Federer and Ivan Ljubičić that the two players, having lost all trust in him, spent the better part of the match refereeing it themselves. Ljubičić is now part of Federer's two-man coaching team and has played his part in the Federer Renaissance, so it all worked out fine between them. Mourier's capacity to sow confusion and discord out of nothing boggles the mind. I saw Mourier in Rome in 2013 break Viktor Troicki's brittle hope that the tennis gods were not against him, a hope that's never returned to Troicki, who has stormed the circuit in an irrepressible rage ever since. Mourier has been at this for a long time. No one is safe from his hoodoo.

Anytime you see Mourier on a court there's the possibility that he's been possessed by some specter from some bygone day who lives under the tennis grounds. He makes himself noticed in a tennis match by his sheer will to be noticed, but he does so without any artistry, improvising a reason to speak or be seen time and again simply because the ATP allows him to. Everyone makes mistakes, and Mourier is no exception. But Mourier is consistently the exception. Google him. I dare you. It's not that he's a bad chair umpire, it's that he's bad at being a good chair umpire, meaning he has a difficult time not being part of the story. When a player asks him why he would make such a horrendous call, he should just shrug like the drowning scorpion and say it's his nature. And now here he comes when absolutely no one asked him to, approaching Goffin's baseline at a crucial moment in the first set of the semifinals in Monaco. It is his nature.

Cédric Mourier missing the mark. Monte Carlo, 2017. (Photograph by Clive Brunskill / Getty Images)

The ball was out. The line judge made the call clearly and instantly. If the chair umpire has a doubt, then the line judge is there to confer with: *Where did you see the mark? Show me.* Instead, Mourier walks to the baseline, picks one of any number of random spots along the line, points to it, and overrules the call. Before he overrules the call, you can see Goffin come over to where Mourier is, curious as to what he's up to, and start to remonstrate that Mourier isn't looking anywhere near where the ball landed. Mourier doesn't have any idea what he's doing at this point. He might as well be looking for the penny someone just tossed into a public fountain.

So, if Mourier had come to Goffin's baseline certain that he had seen something and now is having his conviction put in doubt, this would be a good time to double back and do what he ne-glected to do in the beginning: bring the line judge over. Unlike a chair umpire, line judges can't just insert themselves in these matters. Mourier likes this part. He'll make something up. He'll be proven wrong. But he may shrug and say he saw what he saw and everyone makes mistakes. It's likely. Of course, he'd say this in the restricted lounges of the Monte Carlo Country Club where these things don't matter. Umpires don't give interviews. They only speak publicly via their decisions on the court. They're ghosts in the tennis machine.

And so Goffin, who had survived a stern Nadal challenge in his service game, has suddenly come face-to-face with the long con of the curse. In tennis you have to withstand errors, because errors happen; sometimes they are coaxed out of you, sometimes you make them on your own. But this was something from a different di-mension. You've pushed the boulder far up the hill, and sud-denly, against the laws of nature themselves, it starts to roll back at you. Why was Mourier there on the court when he wasn't asked? Why, if he had seen the ball in, did he not simply overrule it from his chair like any chair umpire in that position would? Why didn't he ask for help when he clearly did not see what he thought he had seen? Goffin was beside himself; he called for the tournament supervisor to come out to the court and intervene. The supervisor did the former but not the latter. The chair umpire, he would ex-plain, had made his call. They had to play on. Out of options, Goffin was left to return to re-enter the point from where things were. Ahead 3–2 in the first, Goffin already with a break and look-ing to consolidate it with a hold: after five deuces, it's advantage Goffin, one point from 4–2.

The game would go on for a second eternity. It would last a total of a staggering seventeen minutes, with the crowd through all of it vocal in their utter disgust at what they'd seen. Nadal just waited for it to be resolved. After the match there were suggestions that, as he clearly acted as though he accepted that the ball had landed out, he should have given the point and hence the game to Goffin. It's been done before, and there are things that happen less frequently on a tennis court. Nadal bristled at this suggestion, and who can blame him? It's not in his makeup: he cherishes every ball and every point like a treasure to hoard. When Mourier pulled a Mourier on him in Madrid, he was up 6–2, 3–1, 40–40, and he treated Mourier's mistake like it was match point in a tiebreaker in the final set. It's not in his nature to give a point away, nor is it his job. When he finally broke Goffin and won the game, the match had balanced at three-games-all, but it felt over. The life had been sucked out of it, or at least the life that it had had been sucked out of it. Goffin had been broken, and he was broken. It was 3–3 in the first, but he would go on to win a grand total of one game for the rest of the match. When you pull back and look over the course of the clay season, Rafa rules over everything, even Rome, where in losing right before the French Open he proved himself human on the clay. Meanwhile, what could have been going through Goffin's head? Mourier had inserted himself into a great match at the asking of absolutely no one, as though he had thought, *This isn't supposed to be part of Rafa's story.* That the clay was a story already written, it just needed to be told. Don't we all want to see history made? Did Cédric Mourier put on his navy blue blazer that day thinking he was going to play his small part in history? After all, all that was going to happen during the circuit's clay-court season—the clay swing— were minor matters until the end, which would be a celebration of the King of Clay. With the state Djokovic and Murray were in and Federer nowhere to be seen, didn't everyone know it? Didn't Cédric Mourier know it? On one side of his court was the King of Clay dressed in purple. And on the other side was a pawn, dressed in an orange that blended into the dirt so much he was almost invisible.

It started out promising, but the end of David Goffin's clay season was swift and heartbreaking. June 2, 2017, Paris, France. (Photograph by Jimmy Bolcina / Photonews / Getty Images)

Afterward, Goffin would go on to have an unremarkable rest of the clay season. Fine but nothing special: a sleepy round-of-sixteen loss to the fifty-sixth-ranked six-foot-six Karen Khachanov in Barcelona, a quarterfinal defeat to the six-foot-one Nadal in Madrid, and a round-of-sixteen loss in Rome to the six-foot-six Marin Čilić. Business as usual, more or less. He had taken the best shot of the curse and he had emerged from it relatively unscathed.

That is, until Paris.

Up 5–4 in the third round against Argentina's Horacio Zeballos and serving for the first set, Goffin somehow saw three opportunities to win set point escape him and suddenly found himself in the middle of a long baseline battle simply to hold serve. The set went from being practically salted away to being in dangerous flux. The rally went on: nine shots . . . eleven . . . thirteen . . . and then on the fourteenth, he had to chase a ball deep to his left way into the back corner of the court. He tripped over a tarp that's kept there to cover the court overnight or in case of bad weather. His ankle gave out under him. Unable to put any pressure on it, he had to be carried off the clay to the medical room. His French Open was over. And he'd miss all of the grass season as well: no Wimbledon.

Don't think I'd end this part of the story here. David Goffin was doomed, yes. Something in the dirt got to him. There was a little bit of the man pushing the rock up the hill to his tale. And a little bit of the power flying too close to someone's sun. Or, he was simply screwed. Permitted incompetence got him at the start of the season, and old-fashioned bad luck got him in the end. Six weeks out and still no titles since 2014, he was a casualty of the clay. But when he came back for the hard courts and beat Kyrgios to help Belgium get past Australia to play in its first Davis Cup final and won the title in Shenzhen and the title in Tokyo, qualified for the end-of-the-year ATP Final, and beat Nadal in the round robin and Federer in the semis before losing the final, once again as in January, to Dimitrov, he ended the season for the first time ever as a top-ten player.

When I look back and wonder what cured him of the curse, how he shook free of it, I find myself remembering what was taken from him in Monte Carlo but also what was given back to him in Paris, which was far stronger and clearly lasted far longer. With his ankle in the condition it was in, Goffin needed immediate medical attention and had been taken straightaway off the court. It was clear that Zeballos, who was losing, had suddenly won. He was the sixty-fifth-ranked player in the world, without a French Open match win to his name since 2013. He had just turned thirty-two and now was into the fourth round of a major, as far by a long shot as he'd ever advanced. It was the obligation of proper decorum more than joy that led Zeballos to wave for a brief moment to the crowd, his hands barely reaching the height of his shoulders. Then he went over to Goffin's chair, where all of his stuff sat unattended, and he packed up everything that was there, every single belonging that might have belonged to him.

He did this first. And then, with Goffin's bag on his back, he packed his own—the towels, extra shirts, etc.—and walked off the court carrying both bags, one on each shoulder, to applause he didn't look like he at all wanted. There's a door in the tunnel to the right just after you exit the court: the trainer's room. Somewhere in there was a hobbled David Goffin. And just outside that door was where Horacio Zeballos of Mar del Plata, Argentina, left the bag for the Belgian, as if to say that when he was ready the sport would be there waiting for him.

THE ROLAND-GARROS EPILOGUE

Rafa Nadal won the 2017 French Open without losing a single set. He had now won ten French Opens. And counting.

The principal court of Roland-Garros, a sea of orange and green, is where the biggest matches are played. And although it's the smallest stadium of the four Grand Slam show courts in terms of audience capacity, the court itself is as spacious as they come. There's room to roam behind and around the sides of the court like few in the world. And the absence of a roof overhead only enhances the feeling of wide-open space. For a player like Nadal, who loves to play deep behind the baseline and range far and wide

RANKING	MOVE	PLAYER	AGE	POINTS	TOURN PLAYED	POINTS DROPPING
1	–	Andy Murray	30	9,890	18	500
2	^2	Rafael Nadal	31	7,285	15	0
3	–	Stan Wawrinka	32	6,175	20	0
4	v2	Novak Djokovic	30	5,805	16	0
5	–	Roger Federer	35	4,945	13	180
6	–	Milos Raonic	26	4,450	21	300
7	^1	Marin Čilić	28	4,115	22	180
8	v1	Dominic Thiem	23	3,985	27	180
9	–	Kei Nishikori	27	3,830	20	45
10	–	Alexander Zverev	20	3,070	24	300
11	–	Jo-Wilfried Tsonga	32	3,040	18	0
12	^1	Grigor Dimitrov	26	2,980	23	0
13	v1	David Goffin	26	2,785	25	0
14	–	Tomáš Berdych	31	2,570	22	0
15	^1	Gaël Monfils	30	2,545	16	0
16	^1	Lucas Pouille	23	2,365	22	0
17	^4	Pablo Carreño Busta	25	2,360	26	0
18	v3	Jack Sock	24	2,335	20	0
19	v1	Roberto Bautista Agut	29	2,155	24	90
20	v1	Nick Kyrgios	22	2,110	20	0

Official ATP rankings, June 12, 2017. (www.atpworldtour.com)

to defend and transition to attack, this clay court is heaven on earth.

Since 2001, this court has been called Court Philippe Chatrier, in honor of the longtime president of the Fédération Française de Tennis. For seventy-three years prior to the renaming, it had been called simply Court Central.

I don't anticipate the French removing Chatrier's name from the stadium. That's not the way things are done. But when all's said and done, some form of memorial to what we've been witnessing at Roland-Garros, the sheer audacity of it, has to happen.

I watched the three-set final against Stan Wawrinka and saw the Swiss play as good a match as I'd see him play this year. And yet he lost, 6–2, 6–3, 6–1. Sometimes a scoreline can make you doubt your senses or, worse, make you seem a liar. Clay swallows winners and spits them back at the player who hit them. Nadal is the best there's ever been at this on this surface. He masters space and time in that stadium like none other. There are no words for what Nadal can do to an opponent on Philippe Chatrier. It's as though he doesn't beat you, he erases you. All the games become one game, all the opponents become one opponent who tries and fails to bend the space and pace of Roland-Garros to his will.

It all happened so fast. There was a French Open in 2017.

And then there wasn't.

In the end, there was only Rafa Nadal.

PART THREE Summer

450 WORDS ON THE AEGON INTERNATIONAL IN EASTBOURNE

Of the top seeds at the 2017 Aegon International in Eastbourne, England, only one was ranked in the top fifteen. The fourth-ranked player in the world entered the ATP 250 tournament late by way of a wild-card invitation. "This will be my first trip to East-bourne. I have heard great things about the tournament," he said. And then, in an echo of Andy Murray's comments when the clay season was about to begin, "I am looking forward to fine-tuning my grass court game ahead of Wimbledon." And with that, East-bourne welcomed its big four to the tournament: fourth-seed Steve Johnson, third-seed John Isner, second-seed Gaël Monfils, and the top-seed Novak Djokovic. It was the first time Djokovic had played on the grass between the end of the French Open and the start of Wimbledon since 2010. It had come to this: desperate times and desperate measures.

Even the idea in January that by June Djokovic would be ranked fourth would have seemed preposterous. Beyond preposterous.

But after years of keeping pace with the massive points total he had to defend—semifinals and finals ad infinitum year after year—in June 2017 he suddenly discovered the other side of being as good as he's been. The year prior, he had won the Australian Open, Indian Wells, Miami, and the French Open, but in 2017 he didn't get far in any of them. And while his point total nosedived, Federer and Nadal took up all of the slack. That's how he found himself at a tournament he never puts on his calendar, Eastbourne, doing something before Wimbledon that he had thought he had long since outgrown: warming up.

Aside from a second-set tiebreaker against the American Donald Young, Djokovic didn't suffer much on the grass and even won that tiebreaker 11–9 and the match in straight sets. In fact, he didn't lose a set. Monfils, perhaps spent from a long back-and-forth semifinal against his countryman Richard Gasquet, once again didn't put up too much of a fight in the final; Djokovic won 6–3, 6–4. There weren't too many conclusions to draw from it. After all, no matter what type of form one or the other is in, Djokovic always beats Monfils. And a draw of Vasek Pospisil, Young, Daniil Medvedev, and a final against Monfils was more to test the body than the mind. He looked okay. No worse for wear than he appeared at the French Open. Five matches later, on No. 1 Court in Wimbledon, his season would be over. He made it through fifteen games against Berdych before his elbow left him in no condition to play. He'd end the season ranked twelfth in the world.

THE FALL AND RISE OF ROGER FEDERER

The year 2016 ended for Roger Federer on Friday, July 8. In the fifth set of his semifinal match at Wimbledon, he found himself sprawled out along his service line, facedown, ruefully lifting his left leg slightly up and slowly letting it back down, as if to prove to the shocked and silent crowd that he was still alive.

Even when he had been ahead in the match against Milos Raonic of Canada, Federer looked weary. In the fourth set, he double-faulted not once but twice, ending any hope for a classic. Raonic—six feet five inches of muscle topped with a Clark Kent hairdo—is an elite-grade version of the typical North American thumper: a thunderous serve, a strong but finicky forehand, and a two-handed backhand right out of an instruction manual; yet he approaches the net like it's an electric fence. Federer had spent his career feasting on this type of player.

But not lately. He hadn't won a title all season; he had knee surgery earlier in the year; he skipped the French Open entirely. These days he seemed more gaunt than gracile, more canny than casually assured. Now and then, he would see what the other player didn't, couldn't. At such moments—whether half volleys in 2015 or overhead backhand smashes in 2014—his fans rejoiced in their nostalgia. David Foster Wallace's Federer essay would make the rounds on the Internet like uncorked champagne.* For those of us his age, who grew up with Marlon Brando in *Superman*, Alec Guinness in *Star Wars*, and Laurence Olivier in *Clash of the Titans*, it was familiar and fine, though we didn't know why. He slowed, but slowed like a dangerous panther. He staged strange suicide missions to the net on his opponents' second serves. His game—a sexy hybrid of tennis in black-and-white, tennis in standard definition, and tennis in 3-D—looked good in defeat. Other players grunted, lunged, sprinted into swinging splits, found the worn

---

*David Foster Wallace's "Roger Federer as Religious Experience" originally appeared in *The New York Times*' short-lived *Play* magazine on August 20, 2006, and has been subsequently collected in *String Theory: David Foster Wallace on Tennis* (New York: Library of America, 2016).

patch on a grass surface to buckle over, the drizzle-slicked white line to slip on. Not Federer. In his tennis dotage, he was like a Fabergé egg spinning on a tabletop because it could.

And then at Wimbledon he fell. And he didn't just fall. He looked like your uncle doing the robot and having it all go wrong. If you saw that match live, you knew then that it was over.

Except it wasn't. He started off the 2017 season ranked seventeenth in the world. Since then, he'd won thirty-one matches and lost two. He skipped Paris again this year, not because of injury but because he could afford to. Clay wears on the body, and besides, why let Rafa Nadal take your measure on his sovereign surface? Instead, Federer took time off and waited for Wimbledon like Christmas morning.

By the time he got there, he was seeded fourth. He looked sharp, dangerous, healthy, his game kaleidoscopic. At the start of week two, Djokovic, the second seed, withdrew with an injured arm. Nadal lost to thirty-four-year-old Gilles Müller and the defending champion, Andy Murray, succumbed in the quarters to American Sam Querrey and a bad hip. Suddenly Federer's 2017 Wimbledon became something else entirely. It became a revenge tour.

Federer cruised to the quarterfinals, where he faced Raonic again. Raonic dug in, threw everything he had at Federer, and still lost in straight sets. In the semifinal, Federer faced the player who had knocked him out of the 2010 Wimbledon quarterfinal, Tomáš Berdych. This time, Federer gut-checked him to the duck-season-duck-season-rabbit-season tune of 7–6 (7–4), 7–6 (7–4), 6–4. After the match, Berdych was asked if the 2017 version of Federer is better than the 2010, to which he replied, "There is no way to prove this, if we can measure it, if he's better or not. He's playing just too good."

In the final, Federer again faced Čilić, who had beaten him in the 2014 U.S. Open. He went the entire tournament without losing a single set. Čilić wept after the second set, realizing that the foot blister he carried over from his semifinal hadn't magically healed. Blister or no, he had no clear path to attacking Federer, and Federer knew it. The pinprick-sized holes in Federer's game, the ones that Nadal and Djokovic learned to pry open, seemed gone now. But that's not to say Federer healed both his body and his game. He seemed to have healed his body and changed his game.

Tennis is a kinetic and rather lonely kind of problem solving. How do you solve for Federer? Serve as though your life depends on it, push him back with high balls to his backhand, make him not only play but also think defensively, and, if any of those happen to work, floor it and don't look back. But he pushes back as hard now as he ever has when he gets a second serve to his backhand. He hits the backhand with topspin and space resolutely from the baseline, exclusively from the baseline, as though he'd been told the world was flat and ended there. So much so that any ball that bounces at the baseline, the type of ball that even a professional would sensibly take a few steps back to hit at knee level, he plays as a difficult half volley that he makes look easy; to hit these with intention, in rhythm, again and again against top professionals, should be practically unthinkable, and yet they have become typical rally strokes in his game. Every point is about finding the first strike as soon as possible. He takes no time between serves. Rather strangely at his age, he has sped things up while making the court smaller. It is his younger opponents—a chagrined Čilić but the latest—who seem starved for time and space.

The following day, Monday, July 17, 2017, a sixteen-year-old boy will appear before a judge in Stratford Youth Court, deep inside an angular beige and burnt sienna building squeezed onto a curving East London city block. He is facing fifteen charges:

RANKING	MOVE	PLAYER	AGE	POINTS	TOURN PLAYED	POINTS DROPPING
1	–	Andy Murray	30	7,750	18	0
2	–	Rafael Nadal	31	7,465	15	0
3	–	Roger Federer	35	6,545	14	0
4	–	Novak Djokovic	30	6,325	17	1,000
5	–	Stan Wawrinka	32	6,140	20	360
6	–	Marin Čilić	28	5,075	23	10
7	–	Dominic Thiem	23	4,030	27	10
8	–	Kei Nishikori	27	3,740	20	600
9	–	Milos Raonic	26	3,310	21	180
10	–	Grigor Dimitrov	26	3,160	23	180
11	–	Alexander Zverev	20	3,070	23	10
12	–	Jo-Wilfried Tsonga	32	2,805	19	0
13	^1	David Goffin	26	2,605	25	90
14	^1	Tomáš Berdych	31	2,570	23	180
15	^1	Pablo Carreño Busta	26	2,350	25	0
16	v3	Gaël Monfils	30	2,275	18	360
17	^1	Lucas Pouille	23	2,255	23	45
18	^1	Roberto Bautista Agut	29	2,245	24	0
19	v2	Jack Sock	24	2,245	19	90
20	^1	John Isner	32	2,045	23	45

Official ATP rankings, July 24, 2017. (www.atpworldtour.com)

one count of possession of an item to discharge a noxious substance, one count of grievous bodily harm with intent, five counts of attempted grievous bodily harm with intent, three counts of robbery, four counts of attempted robbery, and one count of handling stolen goods. He has been accused of spending this past Thursday evening throwing acid onto food deliverymen and making off— or trying to make off—with their vehicles as the victims screamed in agony, unsure of what had just happened to them, why, or what to do. Five times in little over an hour these attacks happened.

Hackney, Islington, Stoke Newington. Neighborhoods in North East London, the other side of the Thames from Wimbledon, where the royal box is empty, the dirt patches are being re-sodded, and we were regally entertained.

Over on No. 3 Court on the first day of Wimbledon, the most talented player in the draw not named Roger Federer is down two sets to love and lying down on the grass, prone on his back, looking up and either squinting from the sun or wincing in pain. He had requested medical assistance and now the trainer was out on the court trying to stretch out his hip. He had lost the first two sets by respectable scores, 3–6, 4–6, to a respectable opponent, Pierre-Hugues Herbert, a two-time Grand Slam champion in doubles, whose game in singles grows on grass the way Albert Ramos Viñolas's game grows on clay. He knew this and would say as much after the match, which would end soon because he couldn't play on. It would surprise no one. He was clearly not fit. Since the circuit had switched from clay to grass he had only played one match, which he lost. And by his own admission his preparation had been less than adequate. He's not alone in preferring to practice lightly. Federer has made it clear for years now that practice is a necessary evil he more endures than enjoys. It's Rafa who feasts off practice. So he'd had a bit of a hit with a friend and played some practice points. His hip had been hurting him, making practice even more perfunctory than it normally was. Andy Murray was also slowed by a bad hip—it was becoming more and more of a known thing. Murray's game hadn't fallen off a cliff, anyone could see that. But the more he soldiered on, the more the problem became clear to anyone watching. The difference was that Andy needed his hips first and foremost so that he could chase down every ball; on the other hand, he used his hips to generate the tremendous power he had on his groundstrokes and serve. That said, regardless of what type of player you may be, the hips are at the center of everything. He had retired from matches before with injuries cited that were harder to see than the lack of effort that came with them. This wasn't the case here. And why would it be? His game was tailor-made for the grass: a thunderous, variable serve; quick feet; power off both wings with little in the way of windup; and soft hands coupled with a natural tactical aggression that together facilitate a smooth and effective net game. He had beaten Nadal here already. On Wimbledon's show court, no less. At the age of nineteen. And barely a year into his professional career. It was the first time they had played each other: he was a teenager gifted a wild card and Nadal was the number-one-ranked player in the world. Thirty-seven aces later (in only four sets and against one of the great returners of serve in the history of the game), even the casual watchers knew his name, the kid who jumped up and down when he got a break of serve, the one who in the middle of a rally hit an inexplicable between-the-legs fore-hand winner from the baseline and asked the Centre Court crowd to celebrate it with him, the brown-skinned Australian guy with the Greek last name, big gold chain, and that little bit of baby fat lingering on his long limbs and face. Three years later, despite the consistency of his inconsistent results and effort and decorum and health, he was the twentieth-ranked player in the world and every-one's dark horse for the 2017 Wimbledon title, even for those who'd already grown tired of his act. But the grass and Herbert and he himself would have none of it. They all conspired together to do Nicholas Hilmy Kyrgios in.

Every form of entertainment, just like every art, has its enfant terrible. Tennis is no exception. Tennis is a sport that aspiring pro-fessionals begin before the age of ten and leaves you isolated to deal with four opponents at once—your opponent, the ball, the net, and yourself—with your parents watching, the other player's parents watching, too many other people watching or too few. It's also a sport that draws you away from other sports, eventually. While football players also can play basketball and run track, young tennis players pursuing a life in the game have to choose tennis exclusively to get in the required reps and open up their schedule for the required travel. Then there's the obvious issue of tennis often not being a sport that an elite tennis player has chosen but a sport that has been chosen for them. Unfortunately, too many parents love to live out their failed fantasies of tennis excellence through their children. Some of these parents simply weren't any good at it, or weren't good enough, or discovered the game late, and reason that if their child gets up at the crack of dawn and hits hundreds of balls each day instead of going to school, then that child will be a great tennis player because it's that easy, and although the parent didn't do that, if he or she or they had a little more luck on their side, someone to really push them, they would most definitely have been a great tennis player. For some parents, it's the easiest way to imagine climbing a social rung or two or twenty-two. And for some others, those whose social life centers on a tennis club, the top-dog status of the child is the top-dog status of the parent. Add to this the cost of things: strings, shoes, a coach, court fees, travel. Add to this the centripetal force of tennis culture, that the life is so particular, the pathway to being a professional is so narrow, its wall impermeable not for others who want to seep in but for those who might want to seep out—and the world becomes by and large a cluster of repeated conditions and symptoms: the Tennis Parent and the Brat being at the top of the list.

So the elephant in the room concerning what people think about Nick Kyrgios when he . . .

- Barely goes through the motions during an opponent's service game after already having been cited for on-court obscenity and racket smashing in earlier matches at

Wimbledon in 2015, one year after his incredible debut there.

- Tells Stan Wawrinka in 2015 at Toronto during a change-over that Kyrgios's good friend and fellow tennis player Thanasi Kokkinakis had "banged [Wawrinka's] girlfriend," leading to a fine and a long suspension.
- Blatantly gives a match away at the Shanghai Masters to Mischa Zverev in an impossible-to-imagine time of forty-eight minutes, so that he received another fine.
- Indulges in a gratuitous fit of racket-smashing here.
- Offers journalists nuggets such as "I played eighteen matches last year and probably tanked eight of them, but I'm still ranked in the top twenty."
- Indulges in a gratuitous fit of racket-smashing there.
- Rarely, if ever, passes on the opportunity to express his ambivalence about the sport.
- Lets loose a full-volume buckshot of expletives at himself, spectators, ball kids, whomever . . .

Kyrgios is clearly bored. He's not bored when he plays Federer, Nadal, Djokovic, or Murray. Adrenaline, opportunity, and pride run through the veins then. But aside from that? He loves basketball, he's passionate about it. He ended up being better at tennis. Let's leave his parents out of this and say that tennis chose him. He hates to train and he hates to travel, the alpha and omega of being an elite tennis player; but let's just say that tennis chose him. He and tennis are at odds. And he lashes out at it. There's not much in the way of sympathy or empathy that comes his way from people who have paid to see a proper match and, let's be honest, aren't inclined to root for him anyway because he is brown, and recalcitrant is not what the people who pay top dollar for a Grand Slam or Masters 1000 in search of a tennis experience are looking for.

Foolish but not stupid, he must sense this, because it looks like he carries this dark cloud often to the court with him. Therefore, instead of being antagonized, he chooses to be the antagonist. He made himself unlikable before most of the world had a chance to choose whether to like or dislike him.

Most of this is too obvious to have had, for the moment, any other outcome. The thing is, and here's the elephant in the room, we've seen this before. Tennis has had more enfants terribles, bad apples, and brats than you can count. Just off the top of my head, there's been Pancho Gonzales, Dennis Ralston (who was coached by Gonzales), Ilie ("Nasty") Năstase, Cliff Richey, Jimmy Connors, John McEnroe, Andre Agassi, Andy Roddick, Marat Safin, Ernests Gulbis, Viktor Troicki, Bernard Tomic—and those were the ones who were good enough to stick around and actually win matches. Richey never won a Grand Slam, but he won twenty-eight singles titles while suffering from alcoholism and depression. Bad behavior is so ingrained in what tennis is that there's even a mockumentary about it: Aaron Williams as played by Andy Samberg in HBO's *7 Days in Hell*. Williams's look is early Agassi—he was a player who most clearly wore, literally, his antagonism—but the character is an amalgam, he is the golem of tennis's long history of fucking children up.

Therefore, Nick Kyrgios is boring.

Not the player, the player who plays: he's brilliant. And the behavior, honestly, who am I to judge? There is the rare exception in professional tennis, but let's face it, most of these people had their childhoods hijacked. They say the right things about it, about their parent-coach who monitors where they go and what they eat, they say their dream has been to be number one in the world since they were a child.

—Etc.

—Etc.

These are, of course, the right things to say. And the right things to say are often the things you don't end up hearing, because you, as the listener, neither care nor believe them. When a player's parent was a coach and the older sibling also plays, you don't care that the player says he or she has always wanted to be a tennis player; you care that they don't say anything but that. So when Gulbis, for example, says to *L'Équipe*, "I respect Roger, Rafa, Novak, and Murray but, for me, all four of them are boring players. Their interviews are boring. Honestly, they are crap. I often go on YouTube to watch the interviews. With tennis, I quickly stop. It is a joke," he's going rogue in a way that the commentariat has no use for other than to say that he's an asshole and therein their mission is accomplished. There are not many roles in tennis; really only the top twenty players out of a few thousand professionals are even noticed or recognizable at any given time. And if there are so few roles in tennis, you can see how someone like Kyrgios would find himself trapped. He has the game to easily be the best player of his generation, he has abused the presumed successor of that role, Sascha Zverev, repeatedly and impiously. Ironically, he has the game for the role of gentleman champion. But he clearly doesn't want to have anything to do with that. At all. Not at the moment, at least. Tennis greatness seems to be to Kyrgios the equivalent of someone born to surf inheriting a stepfather's manufacturing plant. It's there if he wants it, but . . . nah, bro.

So he acts out. He doesn't want to be there most of the time. He doesn't like tennis. And he probably doesn't like you, because you like tennis. Not only do you like tennis, but you've paid money to come watch him play tennis, and he's already told you he doesn't want to be there, so if anyone's the moron, it's you. He's pissed off at best, bored at worst; and soon enough you will be, too. Iron sharpening iron.

You and Nick. He's bored, you're pissed; he's pissed, you're bored. The rather important difference is that Nick is a kid invested in the vicissitudes of his life, the existential plight of being Nick Kyrgios. But he's a kid in his early twenties, meaning he thinks he's an adult. He thinks he's lived, so he knows things; but also that he needs to live so that he knows things. You are an actual adult, meaning you're old in some manner so that when you say you're old it's met with silence. And you want your relationship with Nick to be like it is with most of the players on the circuit—it's a marriage: you love it, or you fake it, or you get the fuck out.

Nick neither loves it nor fakes it nor gets the fuck out.

He shows up again and again with the same bullshit, which is meaningful to him because it's the part of his life that he can't get back, that feels like it will exist apart from all of the other parts, which is something you sense when you're young but because you're young you tend to act on that sense stupidly. This is the beauty and the utter horror of being young.

But, unlike Nick, you actually like tennis and have watched it all your life. Nick is unique to Nick, but you've seen Nick before. Countless times. Nick bores you. And worse, Nick's tennis-hindered sense of existential dread bores you. I know what you want to say to him: *Come on, Nick, snap out of it, I get it, sometimes it sucks, but you've got an A++ game, you've split your two games against Roger, you've won two of five against Rafa (and two of the others were on clay), you've beaten Novak both times you've played him, Murray's swept you in five matches, but come on, man, more of that, please, just practice and stay fit (Federer hates to practice, too), just practice and stay fit, beat who's in front of you, and everything else, happiness, the meaning of it all, even more riches, all of it will take care of itself. Just ball out, man, please, this is getting old, Nick, I know it's your life, but this isn't even original, it's just typical tennis stuff, and you want to be better than that, right? Right, so . . .*

You want to hand him Agassi's autobiography, *Open*. And

I have it on good authority that he hasn't read it. You think he might realize that thirty years ago it was the same old thing. And that NBA players don't get to rebel by sulking because there's the bench waiting for their asses if they do. Nick gives you the Fisher-Price My First Tantrum version of it all. Which he can, because he's alone. There's no one to bench him. No teammate to disappoint. In fact, he's said more than once that he thrives in team tennis situations like the Davis Cup and the Laver Cup because the level of personal responsibility extends to teammates, and he doesn't want to let them down. At some point, likely when he was quite young, he scanned the crowd of a match he was playing in and realized that they were not his teammates and never would be. Federer has made hay off of the crowd. Nadal, too, in a different, more visceral way. Murray knows which few crowds are his (Wimbledon, London) and locks in on them. Djokovic panders incessantly with post-match witticisms, impersonations, physical comedy, and a wincingly forced post-victory routine he does with (or to) the crowd. I can imagine Nick not wanting any of these options, as he doesn't have Federer's learned reserve, Nadal's fountains of energy, Murray's one-of-us pipeline to the people, or Djokovic's inherent need to be loved. So he passes.

At the heart of it all, Nick does what Nick does because he can get away with it. After Shanghai, Malaysia Airlines dropped him as a sponsor. Kids don't buy plane tickets. He's still sponsored by the headphone company Beats, Nike, and the racket equipment company Yonex: three companies that thrive right in the sweet spot of the young, who are sold less on excellence than on the idea of rebellion, especially the safe tempest-in-a-teacup type of rebellion that's long been part and parcel of the game of tennis. He never strikes me as someone who doesn't want to grow older and wiser, he strikes me as someone who doesn't want it to be tennis that makes him grow older and wiser.

Autumn is around the corner. It's always closer than it seems when we're in the thick of Wimbledon. There will be one last Grand Slam in 2017, and Kyrgios will show up in New York—a city ready to understand him like none other on the circuit—and he will lose in the first round to fellow Australian, 235th-ranked John Millman. He'll pick up a code violation for cursing and receive his fair share of visits from the medical trainer. After his exit he'll explain that he's been suffering from right-arm stiffness, that his arm would go numb whenever he hits his serve. Allergic to being coached and having gone without a coach since 2015, Kyrgios is asked if he's going to continue with the arrangement he's had since May with former world number four Sébastien Grosjean. "I don't know, honestly," he sighs. "I'm not good enough for him. You know, he's very dedicated. He's an unbelievable coach. He probably deserves a player that is more dedicated than I am. There are players out there that are more dedicated, that want to get better, that strive to get better every day, the one-percenters. I'm not that guy."

By the beginning of the 2018 season Kyrgios will again be on the circuit without a coach—and he'll start the year winning Brisbane.

PART FOUR **Fall**

THE U.S. OPEN

D.C. is done.

Montreal is done.

The small clay-court tournaments in Båstad, Umag, Hamburg, Gstaad, and Kitzbühel, the ones that linger on the calendar long after the clay season has ended, are all done.

Cincinnati is done.

Winston-Salem, too.

It's late August. The 2017 season is thirty-four weeks old—and, my, how things have changed.

The passing weeks and the momentum of the months have given clarity and an unexpected form to the year.

After Wimbledon, an Atlanta, then a Los Cabos: the circuit surges forward. Welcome to the second half of the season's second act—the less romantic, more pragmatic part of year, when the names of cell phone companies, insurance companies, and banks are superimposed on one tournament venue after another, causing

RANKING	MOVE	PLAYER	AGE	POINTS	TOURN PLAYED	POINTS DROPPING
1	–	Andy Murray	30	7,750	19	600
2	–	Rafael Nadal	31	7,555	16	90
3	–	Roger Federer	36	7,145	15	0
4	–	Stan Wawrinka	32	5,780	19	90
5	–	Novak Djokovic	30	5,325	16	0
6	–	Marin Čilić	28	5,155	22	1,000
7	ʌ1	Alexander Zverev	20	4,470	24	10
8	v1	Dominic Thiem	23	4,030	28	180
9	–	Kei Nishikori	27	3,385	21	90
10	–	Milos Raonic	26	3,230	22	360
11	–	Grigor Dimitrov	26	3,070	24	360
12	–	Jo-Wilfried Tsonga	32	2,770	20	90
13	–	David Goffin	26	2,560	26	45
14	ʌ2	Roberto Bautista Agut	29	2,425	25	10
15	v1	Tomáš Berdych	31	2,390	24	90
16	ʌ1	Jack Sock	24	2,325	21	0
17	v2	Pablo Carreño Busta	26	2,305	25	10
18	–	Lucas Pouille	23	2,220	24	10
19	–	John Isner	32	2,110	23	45
20	–	Sam Querrey	29	2,060	23	10

Official ATP rankings, August 14, 2017. (www.atpworldtour.com)

courts that already look strikingly similar to sound so as well. In 2016, the 250 tournament in scenic Los Cabos debuted, having doubled down with a bank and a media chain in its choice of name: Abierto Mexicano de Tenis Mifel presentado por Cinemex. Wikipedia just called it the Los Cabos Open.

The truth is that even the big fish in this group—the Citi Open in D.C., the Coupe Rogers/Rogers Cup in Montreal/Toronto, the Western & Southern Open in Cincinnati—fight for our attention amid the spiking heat. The venues fill, but if I'm not around a tennis court the tournaments tend not to come up in conversation, which

RANKING	MOVE	PLAYER	AGE	POINTS	TOURN PLAYED	POINTS DROPPING
1	^1	Rafael Nadal	31	7,645	16	0
2	v1	Andy Murray	30	7,150	18	0
3	_	Roger Federer	36	7,145	16	0
4	_	Stan Wawrinka	32	5,690	18	0
5	_	Novak Djokovic	30	5,325	17	0
6	^1	Alexander Zverev	20	4,470	24	0
7	v1	Marin Čilić	28	4,155	22	0
8	_	Dominic Thiem	23	4,030	28	0
9	^2	Grigor Dimitrov	26	3,710	24	0
10	v1	Kei Nishikori	27	3,195	21	0
11	v1	Milos Raonic	26	2,870	22	0
12	_	Jo-Wilfried Tsonga	32	2,690	20	0
13	_	David Goffin	26	2,525	26	0
14	^5	John Isner	32	2,425	23	0
15	v1	Roberto Bautista Agut	29	2,425	25	150
16	^1	Pablo Carreño Busta	26	2,385	25	250
17	v1	Jack Sock	24	2,345	21	0
18	^5	Nick Kyrgios	22	2,325	20	0
19	v4	Tomas Berdych	31	2,310	24	0
20	v2	Lucas Pouille	23	2,210	24	0

Official ATP Rankings, August 21, 2017. (www.atpworldtour.com)

is a shame, but also the cost of the overwhelming attention that the four Grand Slams bring upon themselves. And so, I usually spend a month or so swimming in a summer fog of these matches waiting for and wondering about the next major. The wait for the U.S. Open can feel interminable. I tide myself over with these other tournaments. And as I have grown older I have learned to love them, too. They are prologues to the U.S. Open, when only late summer remains and, after blazing a trail through more heat and humidity than a person is supposed to bear, the circuit descends upon New York.

With each name etched on a trophy, tournament after tournament after tournament, the long season shortens, leaving a little of itself behind at each place. The tour changes that much more from the dream it once was to the reality it now is and will forever after be. Where once there was a hunch, now there's history; where once there was a feeling, now there's fact. There is no fake news, only what has happened. And what has happened is that for the first time this year, after eight months of circling the globe, the circuit can see in the late-summer haze of the Manhattan skyline not just the sun but an ending.

Seven of the nine Masters 1000s are past.

A player can never get them back. A fan can never get them back. The Australian Open and the French, Miami, and Monaco, all of those matches from earlier in the year—the Indian Wellses, Istanbuls, and Eastbournes—were pushing us forward. What happens, then, when there's less and less space ahead to push forward into?

Three of the four Grand Slams are gone.

What happens when there are fewer and fewer pieces of the puzzle? What happens when you can see what the puzzle is—that it will absolutely be either one thing or the other—and you can even see, despite the gaps, the completeness of it? The year 2017 started with an air of inevitability around the Murray-Djokovic rivalry; it was to be the pivot around which everything on the men's tour turned. Now, in retrospect, the Australian Open wasn't just one of the great surprises of recent tennis history, it was one of the most important tournaments in tennis history as well. Had Federer and Nadal appeared in the Melbourne final in their thirties and then returned to their respective forms of the past few years, the Australian Open would have remained spectacle and iconic entertainment. But the way in which the two of them dominated the 2017 season after Melbourne has changed that Grand

Slam from a memento to a moment of significant change. It gave us the first sight into a future we didn't see coming, even though it was happening right before our eyes. We confused it with the past: Rafa and Roger, like Venus and Serena, dusted off for one final go-around, golden parachutes strapped to their backs.

There's no choice but to think differently about those late nights and early mornings, bingeing on tennis in the dark because the world felt so precarious and you couldn't sleep. They were, as I said earlier, an idea of order. Not an idea of order you would have ever expected in 2017, but an idea of order all the same. You considered it a guilty pleasure, an indulgence of the part of you that loves nostalgia; but it was instead a sign of things to come. You couldn't know it then. But by Indian Wells or Miami, you should have had an inkling. By Barcelona that inkling should have been a bell. And by Wimbledon that bell should have been ringing, this time in your head as much as in your heart. Federer and Nadal had taken every tournament that defines them this year. Zverev could have Montreal and Rome. "Baby Fed" Dimitrov could have Cincinnati. No two players grew more in stature over the course of the year than those two, with Goffin not far behind. But Melbourne, Paris, and Wimbledon—those trophies might as well have *noli me tangere* inscribed across the front for anyone in 2017 not named Rafa Nadal or Roger Federer.

Now it was New York's turn. The extremely public spectacle of Grand Slams—how they tend to bring out the tennis fan in all of us, even if only temporarily—reaches its peak with the final one of the year, when stories come into focus, scores are settled, promises kept or destroyed. This is how the tour descends on the city, not with the glitz and glamour of Broadway, but rather with the feeling of culmination and exhaustion at sunset like a showdown at the end of a western set on a series of hard courts in the borough of Queens.

The U.S. Open is my hometown tournament. I have always wanted it to feel like home, like a warm, inviting, and familiar place with its own local charm. As strange as it may sound, this in its essence has always been New York to me. And yet, I want New York to be the other New York, too. You know which one. Yes, that New York. I want it to be an imposing metropolis, a tough city for tough people with an unshakable sense of itself as the center of the world. This is also, in its essence, New York to me. I want it to be a prism of glass and steel where I can feel lost and alone when I want to; I want to be able to be struck by sudden sadness or joy surrounded by thousands of people and feel that no one is there. This heartens me. New York has always been that city, too. I want all of the New Yorks, together and at the same time. This seems impossible on one hand and a description of every day on the other. No tennis event encapsulates this quite like the U.S. Open, which has been held over the years on all three surfaces—first grass, then clay, now hard courts—at day and at night, outdoors and under a roof; it's been rowdy, it's been pristine; but most of all, regardless of any of this, it's been grand.

CHRONICLE OF A DEATH FORETOLD: ON WHY THE 2017 U.S. OPEN WAS TERRIBLE

When you're walking to the entrance of the U.S. Open from the Mets–Willets Point subway station, it's hard not to think about all that's going on and how life seems to simply go on. But really, what's simple anymore? And what's done simply? I walked on and hundreds of us exited through turnstiles and turned right to head to the Billie Jean King National Tennis Center as hundreds more exited through turnstiles and turned left to head to Citi Field. Normally it's home to the Mets, but this night it was the home of a

Lady Gaga concert. Roosevelt Avenue was flush with traffic, the wheels making slushing sounds in the constant puddle the falling rain spread on the pavement. Jonathan Galassi and I had tickets to see the night matches in Arthur Ashe Stadium and, of course, it has a retractable roof and so, although the remaining outdoor matches were being suspended as afternoon turned to evening and the rain continued to fall, we knew we wouldn't miss anything because the matches we were going to would be played under Ashe's immense dome. The rain didn't matter much. And, free of worry of missing out, we wandered over the wooden-planked overpass that leads to the tennis ground and dreamed a little.

Imagine a 2017 U.S. Open with everyone healthy. The top eight seeds would be some mixture—in no particular order—of Murray, Djokovic, Nadal, Federer, Wawrinka, Raonic, Nishikori, and Čilić. Six of those players have won the U.S. Open and Nishikori is a past finalist. Raonic has only gone as far as the fourth round, but the hard courts suit his game and he's been a recent finalist at Wimbledon and semifinalist at the Australian Open. Each wins his respective section of the draw, and you're left with these eight as your quarterfinalists. Seeding at this point would be everything: who matches up with whom, who doesn't face whom unless they both reach the final. It could have been great, and it was what had been missing from the season. Not everyone had been healthy during any point of the year, aside from possibly during the Australian Open way back in January. It would have been great to see a top eight and then throw in Thiem, Dimitrov, Monfils, Zverev, Goffin, Tsonga, Berdych, players capable of staging an upset and reaching a quarterfinal or semifinal. It could have been great. It likely would have been great. But it wasn't meant to be. Due to his ailing elbow, Djokovic ruled himself out for the rest of the year. After fifty-one straight Grand Slam appearances dating back to 2005, he would miss one. Wawrinka, one Centre Court title away from a career Grand Slam, lost in the first round of Wimbledon and shortly after shut himself down for the rest of the season. Just like that, the U.S. Open lost its defending champion. Raonic, riddled with injuries throughout the year and having seen his ranking drop down to eleventh from third, withdrew from the Open after Montreal due to an injury to his wrist—he would play only one more tournament in the year, Tokyo in October, which he would end up retired from again because of injury. Nishikori would also withdraw due to a need for surgery in his wrist; his team released a statement saying that "during practice in Cincinnati, Kei hit a serve and heard a 'pop' in his wrist." Čilić decided to play, despite missing Montreal and Cincinnati with an abductor injury, but didn't look right at all in his early matches and ended up losing in the third round. Nadal was still standing and grinding out victories after losing first sets, but he, too, was clearly slowing.

It was less than a month ago that he'd lost early in Montreal to eighteen-year-old Canadian phenom Denis Shapovalov and in the quarterfinals of Cincinnati to Kyrgios. What's more, despite now having regained the number-one ranking the very week of the U.S. Open, he hadn't won a hard-court title since Doha all the way back in January 2014. He had managed to reach five finals on the surface since then and he'd lost them all. Federer, meanwhile, tweaked his back in Montreal at some point during his first match since the Wimbledon final. He played and won the next three matches that took him to the final, but looked uncomfortable doing so; during the time between points he seemed pensive, as though he didn't understand the language his body was speaking or, worse, understood it all too well. By the time he played the final in Montreal he was a shell of himself and logged a dutiful sixty-nine minutes on the court before losing the title to the twenty-year-old German Zverev 6–3, 6–4. Over the course of his career Federer's most troublesome nemeses have been Nadal, Djokovic, and his back. It would be wishful thinking to consider him the favorite at the U.S. Open in light of the form he showed in Canada. And so that mantle, through process of elimination, went to the world's number one and the number one seed: Nadal. And if Federer was not fully healthy, which he clearly wasn't, then the rest of the field was open.

And as for Andy Murray, well . . . his biggest impact on the 2017 season was destined to happen in New York over the course of half a day when he decided, just two days prior to the start of the tournament, that he was not going to play.

It was a typical Saturday afternoon. At eleven on Monday morning the U.S. Open was set to begin. In the days leading up to the start, players passed each other on the grounds on their way to and from their practice sessions. Andy Murray hadn't played since Wimbledon on July 12. Trouble with his hips had wrecked his season, with Wimbledon being the worst showing thus far. On the court that turned him into a legend of the game, Wimbledon's Centre Court, he lost the final two sets to Sam Querrey 1–6, 1–6. He'd suffered his share of heartbreak on that court before at the hands of Federer, who in the past had brought him to tears there.

Federer.

He'd beaten Murray in the final in New York in 2008 to win his fifth straight U.S. Open, tying a record for the open era. In 2010, he beat Murray in the final in Melbourne for his fourth Australian Open title, tying a record for the open era. In 2012, Murray became the first British man to play in a Wimbledon final since Henry Wilfred ("Bunny") Austin in 1938. Great Britain whipped itself up into the type of fury usually reserved for every four years when misguided, overenthusiastic optimism about England's chances in the World Cup floods the papers and pubs. The pressure on Murray was stifling, and more so (strangely, not less) after Murray won the first set. Then Federer won the next three on the trot for his seventh Wimbledon singles title, tying him for the most ever with Pete Sampras and our old friend from Cannes, William Renshaw.

But now it was 2017 and Murray was at the ultimate peak of his career. He began Wimbledon as the world number one and the tournament's defending champion, but as those two July weeks went on it became clear to everyone watching that someone would have to answer the call of a resurgent Federer, who was lurking loudly on the other half of the draw. But Murray's body betrayed him before he got that far. The London resident capitulated meekly to Querrey before a squirming local crowd. Those final two sets were difficult to watch. Murray moved like he was wearing flippers. There are more than a fair share of players on the circuit who would have simply conceded the match. But Murray, like Wawrinka in the first round, played it out on hobbled wheels. And in doing so he showed the world just how useless a professional tennis player can look trying to compete in an elite, high-stakes competition against another pro from the upper echelon of the game. He needed to rest and heal. It was possible he needed surgery. It was undeniable he needed to reset.

Murray's tendency after Wimbledon was to only play the two big tournaments before the U.S. Open—the one in Canada and the one in Cincinnati—but this year he skipped them both. This was the first time in his career that he was the number one player in the world, the first time he entered every tournament—Doha, the Australian Open, Indian Wells, even Rafa's Roland-Garros—as the top seed. He'd not only won none of them, he had only reached the finals of the 250 in Doha, where Djokovic beat him in his debut as the world number one with the equivalent of a slap behind the ear from the bigger kid, and the 250 in Dubai, where his opponents were Malek Jaziri (then ranked fifty-first), Guillermo García-López (ninety-seventh), Kohlschreiber (twenty-ninth), Lucas Pouille (fifteenth), and in the final Fernando Verdasco (thirty-fifth).

That was as good as it had gotten on the tennis court for Andy Murray in 2017.

But there was still the U.S. Open.

He looked over the schedule. After the U.S. Open there's the Asian Swing: Chengdu, Shenzhen, Beijing, Tokyo, and the penultimate Masters 1000 of the season in Shanghai. Then the indoor season in Europe, the last Masters 1000 indoors in Paris, and then, closing things out in November, the tour's round-robin tournament back home in London for the top eight players of the calendar year. It was in 2016 in London that Murray had managed to pull off what once seemed impossible: clawing back a massive point differential from Djokovic to close the year at number one. There was no way he'd even make it back to London; he wouldn't have enough points for the year unless he went on the same type of late run he had last year. It was physically impossible for him. But there was still the U.S. Open. He'd won it once before. In fact, it was the first Grand Slam title he won and it remains the only Grand Slam title he has that's not Wimbledon. It was back in 2012, when Berdych beat Federer in the quarterfinals, paving the way for Murray to beat Berdych in the semifinals and, running with the momentum, to beat Djokovic in a five-set final. He was the third seed in that U.S. Open . . . Djokovic was the second seed.

2012. Those were good memories. Much better than those on the court in 2017.

Murray hadn't played in a competitive match in close to two months. At this point he didn't know if he could. But, as Shakira sang, hips don't lie. During practice, after practice, what were they telling him? Could he play in his condition? Was he getting better? Worse? He had 7,150 ranking points, which rather obviously qualified him for direct entry into the U.S. Open. Of course it would. Those are 7,150 points. And he had been the top-ranked player on the circuit from day one of 2017.

QUARTERFINALS | SEMIFINALS | FINAL

1 Roger Federer 6^1 4 6 3
6 Tomáš Berdych 7^7 6 3 6

6 Tomáš Berdych 7 2 1 6^7
3 Andy Murray 5 6 6 7^9

3 Andy Murray 3 7^7 6 6
12 Marin Čilić 6 6^4 2 0

3 Andy Murray 7^{12} 7 2 3 6
2 Novak Djokovic 6^{10} 5 6 6 2

8 Janko Tipsarević 3 7^7 6 3 6^4
4 David Ferrer 6 6^5 2 6 7^7

4 David Ferrer 6 1 4 2
2 Novak Djokovic 2 6 6 6

7 Juan Martín del Potro 2 6^3 4
2 Novak Djokovic 6 7^7 6

The final three rounds of the 2012 U.S. Open.

On Monday the twenty-first of August, a week to the day before the 2017 U.S. Open was set to start, the points accumulated from Nadal's seemingly innocuous loss to Kyrgios in the quarterfinals of Cincinnati were tallied into his total. The number came out to 7,645.

For the first time since June 2014, Rafael Nadal was the world's number one.

Back in January, at the start of the Australian Open, Murray was the proud owner of a monstrous 12,560 points.

That was, at that moment, 9,365 more than Nadal.

And 10,580 more than Federer.

Now he was back to number two. Somehow.

It was unthinkable. And inexplicable.

That day, for the first time since 1918, a total solar eclipse crossed the United States in plain sight from coast to coast. It was called the Great American Eclipse. Scotland was one of the few countries in Europe to see it from beginning to end. Sunset had already come to the rest of the UK by then; they missed the end, they were in the dark. The new number-two-ranked player in the world wondered what he should do.

• • •

He spent that week in New York on the practice grounds hitting as many balls as he could bear over the net. A fundamentalist disciple of practice, Nadal saw him there and reasoned that he would play. Rafa has spent practically half his career having these hard conversations with his body. To play or not to play. Can you play? Should you play? Sometimes you have a breakthrough, you stay in the draw and give it a shot. Sometimes your body doesn't respond and you withdraw. Even Nadal knew that you don't need to have his injury history to know how this goes. The second biggest story of the year on the men's tour had been injuries. People play or they bow out. The U.S. Open had become a veritable graveyard of withdrawn names. It happens. Rafa's been there. Many players, or most, on the circuit have. Can you play? Should you play? Murray let the days pass, practicing and without making further statements one way or the other. Monday turned into Wednesday and Wednesday into Friday, the day of the draw.

Tournaments use the week before they begin for all the brouhaha: press events, social obligations on behalf of the tournament organizers, outreach to the local community, etc. As the week progresses toward the start of play, these whittle down to the announcement of the draw, which is when it's revealed who begins playing whom on the first days of the competition and each player's potential path through the tournament to the finals. You wouldn't do the draw earlier in the week because you don't want to make it a longer distraction on the players' preparation, you want to give players time to assure themselves that they're fit enough to play, and shit happens, so by making the draw on Friday you're giving the players the most time possible to make it through the week without a game-changing setback that would necessitate a late withdrawal. As with all Grand Slam tournaments, there are 128 players in the men's draw at the U.S. Open. Thirty-two seeds.

Putting everything together is logistical origami. A player's fitness can be the monkey wrench in not days or weeks but months of planning. So the draws are announced on Friday, two days prior to the start of the first round. And thus, when the draw reveals the tournament changes, it takes a shape, accepts and rejects possible futures of itself; although far from having an outcome, the tournament has its architecture.

Players with ambitions, then, of going deep in the competition would put head to pillow on Friday night knowing the lay of the land of their section of the draw. And who they would only be able to face in the finals due to the mere fact of having been placed on the opposite half of the draw. For the most part, draws are random. The Austrian Jürgen Melzer is still active, was born the same year as Federer, turned pro in 1999 (Federer in 1998), competed with him in juniors, and has been ranked as high as eighth in the world—Melzer and Federer have played each other five times on the circuit. The American Frances Tiafoe was born in 1998. He cracked the top one hundred for the first time in January 2017. He has a handful of victories on the ATP Tour. Many players in Tiafoe's position won't play Federer even once in their career—he played him three times in 2017 alone, including in a late-night match in the first round of the U.S. Open.

Amid all the possible chaos in a draw is a singular certainty—think of it as the death-and-taxes fact of the thing, the cold, hard truth of why there's even a draw at all—the top two seeds can only play each other in the final. A draw exists to keep the presumed two best players in a tournament as far away from each other and out of each other's way until the presumed showdown at the end. All of the other stuff—the intriguing early matchups, the dark-horse title contenders circling like sharks in some complicated section of the draw, the upsets, feel-good stories, and fairy-tale runs by young up-and-comers making the most of a wild card and by veterans returning to the fray and riding good momentum built on from the grind of the qualifying rounds—all of those are fringe benefits, the light show to keep you busy. A draw has a function. Intriguing first-round matchups and unexpected quarterfinal runs are not functions of design, they're the residue of function. The function of design is to have one and two meet. Hence, the phrase you have likely heard, "if things hold to form." If things hold to form, Player 1 and Player 2 will meet in the final. Form follows function.

The system both rewards and corrects itself. A one and two seed should be good enough to beat the rest of the field, so the draw separates them, provides for that presumption, and the reward for those top two seeds (and for the tournament organizers) is that the two best players face off against each other. If the two players are indeed that far ahead of the rest of the field, their rankings and hence their seedings perpetuate this and the matchup replicates itself again and again, tournament after tournament.

These are the currents swimming under the surface structure of a Grand Slam draw. Even before a tournament starts, once the seed is implemented and the sections are arranged you can read a draw like the box score of a baseball game. It's not just who will win the things—points and positioning suddenly appear before our eyes. The pundits have their ideas of what may happen and express it to the fans. Fans have their ideas of what may happen and express it among themselves. Gamblers have their ideas of what may happen and put money down on it. And the players, the moving pieces in all of this, suddenly have a sense of their possible roles in the drama. Maybe they talk it over with their coaches. Maybe they keep it all to themselves.

But seeding . . . seeding lights up a draw like a Christmas tree.

When the new rankings came out, Murray saw the number two beside his name for the first time in almost a year. He'd worked so hard to shake himself free of it. Wasn't he paying for it now? Hadn't he been paying for it all year? Didn't he all but set fire to his body at the end of 2016 on that impossible and legendary run to become the end-of-the-year number one? The new number-two-ranked player in the world wondered what he should do.

There is nothing mysterious about seeding. Nadal would be the first seed at this U.S. Open, Murray would be two. Federer would be three. Barring the rarest of circumstances, seeding simply follows the tour rankings. At the 2017 Australian Open the top twenty-seven seeds of the tournament corresponded with the rankings of the top-twenty-seven-ranked players in the world. And so, even with so many top players having already withdrawn from the Open, it was easy to know what the seeds going into the 2017 U.S. Open would be. Let's look at the first seventeen seeds.

1. Rafael Nadal (Spain)
2. Andy Murray (UK)
3. Roger Federer (Switzerland)
4. Alexander Zverev (Germany)
5. Marin Čilić (Croatia)
6. Dominic Thiem (Austria)
7. Grigor Dimitrov (Bulgaria)
8. Jo-Wilfried Tsonga (France)
9. David Goffin (Belgium)
10. John Isner (USA)
11. Roberto Bautista Agut (Spain)
12. Pablo Carreño Busta (Spain)
13. Jack Sock (USA)
14. Nick Kyrgios (Australia)
15. Tomáš Berdych (Czech Republic)
16. Lucas Pouille (France)
17. Sam Querrey (USA)

If the seeds of a tournament are a blueprint of hierarchy and expectation, then the expectation on seeing the draw of this U.S. Open was that it was going to be a terrible tournament. Outside Nadal, Murray, and Federer, this was a murderer's row of players who can astound you in one round and absolutely mortify you the next. Even the surging Sascha Zverev, sporting by far his highest-ever seed at a Grand Slam, had never ever made it to the second week of one. His game thus far had been built for best-of-three-set matches and time and time again in his young career he had shrunk before the only true measure of a player's greatness, the demands of best-of-five Grand Slams. Čilić won the U.S. Open in 2014 but since then had played to type as a player just as capable of being upset in an early round as he was of making and losing a semifinal or final. The rest? You could count a few surprise semifinals among them and enough of a track record to be dangerous in a draw but not anyone's idea of a prohibitive favorite. I'm being kind here and I'm not sure why. Tennis is incredibly difficult to play well, and these are a few of the very few finest players in the entire world. This was an eyesore of a seeding chart, and one of the shittiest for a Grand Slam I'd ever seen in my life. Some of the air came out of the U.S. Open when whatever we all knew was put so plainly to see in the plainspoken factness of a list. And the seeds, given the literal luck of the draw, couldn't help but hold to form: Zverev went out in the second round, Čilić in the third. Thiem in the fourth. Dimitrov in the second. Tsonga in the second. Goffin in the fourth. Isner in the third. Bautista Agut in the third. Carreño Busta, enjoying by far the best year of his career, reached the semifinals and then was routined by the twenty-eighth-seeded Kevin Anderson. Jack Sock lost on the first day of the tournament. Kyrgios lost in the first round. Berdych lost in the second round. Pouille lost in the fourth round. Querrey, playing in his home country and with a path to the final he would never in his life have dared to dream of, lost in the quarterfinals to the plucky Anderson in the Battle of Big Servers Who Don't Move Well . . . at All. This wasn't a tournament to dream of a Federer-Nadal matchup, it was a tournament that a Federer-Nadal matchup would have to save.

And if it were to happen, it would have to be in the semifinals. Andy Murray was the second-ranked player in the world. He was the number two seed. If the draw said anything, it was that he and Rafa Nadal were supposed to play in the finals. This was what we wanted. The two best players in the world really going at it. That was his story and he was sticking to it.

The next day Andy Murray withdrew from the 2017 U.S. Open. No one saw it coming. Because no top player withdraws from a tournament after the draw's been made, especially not due to an injury he's been dealing with for months. It throws the draw into utter chaos. He would say he had done pretty much everything he could to get himself ready for New York after taking a number of weeks off after Wimbledon.

"I obviously spoke to a lot of hip specialists," he would continue.

Obviously.

"Tried obviously resting, rehabbing, to try and get myself ready here." Obviously.

"Was actually practicing okay the last few days," he went on, "but it's too sore for me to win the tournament. And ultimately, that's what I was here to try and do."

Murray hadn't re-injured himself, further injured himself, or sustained a new injury. He simply realized that he couldn't win the U.S. Open after not having won a tournament since the first week of March and having been last seen some six weeks ago as a physical shell of himself. Monday, Tuesday, Wednesday, Thursday, watching the draw take an unchangeable diamond form on

Friday, and then announcing the following day that he was unfit to play . . . what to say? If Murray had withdrawn from the tournament just one day earlier, Federer would have simply slipped into the second seed in the other half of the draw from Nadal. But instead, by the rules of the U.S. Open, no one would replace Murray in the number two seed. He was not playing, but he was still number two. Asked about it, Nadal could hardly hide his bemusement, and called it "a little bit strange that he retired just the morning after the draw was made."

Q: Did you get a chance to talk with Andy before he left? Were you surprised to hear that he pulled out, given that you were here and practicing?

RAFAEL NADAL: Yeah, no. I saw him when I arrived here, and I was just saying hi to him.

But I always thought that he was gonna be playing if he was here practicing, no? Was a little bit strange that he retired just the morning after the draw was made. Was something that is a little bit strange and difficult to understand, but the worst thing is, yeah, he is not healthy and I wish him a very fast recovery.

Injuries are bad for everybody. I know better than all of them (*smiling*). So I wish him fast and good recovery. That's the most important thing.

Q: Strange in what way?

RAFAEL NADAL: Strange in what?

Q: You said his decision was strange, the timing of his decision was strange. What do you mean by that?

RAFAEL NADAL: Strange? Yeah, of course. Because normally when you retire on—was Saturday morning? And the draw was made Friday? Normally you want to keep practicing, keep trying until the last moment. You don't retire Saturday morning. You retire Monday morning or Sunday afternoon, not Saturday morning.

If not, you can do it before the draw. That's why I said it's strange. But of course he has his reason, and for sure the negative—the only news and the negative news was that he will not be playing here.

Čilić was moved to Murray's slot in the draw and remained the fifth seed. Kohlschreiber, the first player at the cutoff line for seeding, became the thirty-third seed. There were still only thirty-two seeds: Murray now existing and not existing. Rafa and Roger would have to settle for their semifinal. Maybe one of them would get the 2,000 points from winning the whole thing. But Murray had guaranteed that only one or the other would get the points for reaching the final. Either Rafa or Roger could possibly get a maximum of 720 points from reaching the semifinal. If they both made the final, one was guaranteed 1,200 and the other 2,000. Being in the same side of the draw took 880 points off the table for one of them. Who would know whether that would play out at a later date? Points last for 365 days, give or take a day. So points in play at the U.S. Open would be part of the story in ranking and seeding all the way up to the 2018 U.S. Open. The draw had lost a star extremely late. But the star had already gone; it just took a while for the message to arrive.

Andy Murray left New York with a message that he would announce his plans for the rest of the 2017 season in the following days. It was only going to be one way; he'd been finished since July but fought to deny it. Days later, he confirmed that he was done for the year. It wasn't news as much as recognition of what was already obvious to everyone but him. He needed help. His hips were failing him. It was harder to accept in New York. When he won it all there in 2012 it had marked the first time in five years that Federer and Djokovic had not played each other for the championship. In the final that few saw coming, he started brightly against Djokovic by winning the first two sets as they went down to the wire. Then he lost his way in the third and fourth sets before righting himself and powering past the great Serb in the fifth. He was twenty-five, tireless, and strong. The trophy seemed small in his hands. He knew even back then, especially back then, that the great players in his way were a wall that he would have to break down. He learned how to force his way in. One tournament at a time. He grew accustomed to ruining the expectations of others who expected, at times explicitly wished for, other outcomes. He played the game to be in every final. He had lost eight Grand Slam finals; he knew there was glory in being there.

It was the best-played match Murray would play all year. It brought him to tears.

In January 2018 at 7:30 one morning, he was wheeled into an operating room in Melbourne to have surgery on his hip. He still hadn't played a competitive match since Wimbledon the previous July.

FEDERER VS. TIAFOE

It's the second day of the U.S. Open and late on a Tuesday night that's tumbled over into early Wednesday morning. Arthur Ashe Stadium is still full. Deep into the deciding fifth set, the roof is closed, as it has been all night, causing the constant run-run of idle chatter by tens of thousands in the stands to swell and circle over and around the court as a resigned, halfhearted attempt at silence. Some there were transfixed. Some were simply trapped. New York was experiencing an early taste of bitter autumn. Due to the evening's constant downpour, the uncharacteristically cold gusts of air blasting past the Food Village, and the flooded walkways once lined with concession stands, no one is milling about outside. Sometimes people with a pass to the grounds but not to Ashe would stick around and watch the stadium match on the large screen on the outside wall facing the south plaza. Sometimes there was the simple joy in being a remainder from the daytime matches on the smaller side courts now empty and ignored under the floodlights. All of the day's other matches have been played or washed out and postponed. Two days in, and the tournament was already chasing its tail around—so many stars having withdrawn with injuries, high seeds being eliminated, and the fallout from Andy Murray's manipulation of the draw still being felt. It's dark outside, uncharacteristically dark for New York, where the lights are always on. Midnight blue has given way to cloud rule, a matte black of after-midnight darkness. A darkness that had creeped inside Ashe with all of us, seeping through the white roof suspended high above the single hard court down below at its center and from where several embankments of lights descend down onto the court, leaving an almost-apologetic chrome glaze in the air. It traps the corporate drunkenness in it like heat. Roger Federer readied himself to serve to unseeded nineteen-year-old American Frances Tiafoe from Maryland, two-sets-all, 5–3 in the fifth, 40–all: two points from winning the match but also two points from edging toward disaster. He starts his toss, bends his knees, twists into trophy position, and rises to meet the ball.

Born in January 1998, Frances Tiafoe and his twin brother, Franklin, are the children of immigrants from Sierra Leone, where as a child his father labored in the country's diamond mines. His mother and father, Alphina and Constant, fled the country in the early

Frances Tiafoe of the United States in action against Roger Federer of Switzerland in a five-set first-round match at Arthur Ashe Stadium, August 29, 2017. (Photograph by Mohammed Elshamy / Anadolu Agency / Getty Images)

1990s and settled in Hyattsville, Maryland, one of the constellation of suburbs surrounding Washington, D.C.

Eventually, Constant found a steady job working as a member of the maintenance staff of the Junior Championship Tennis Center in nearby College Park, Maryland. They provided him with an office that he could use as a living space. Alphina worked weekday night shifts as a nurse. And so Monday through Friday, from 1999 until 2010, Frances and Franklin lived with their father, Constant, on the grounds of a suburban tennis center in a 120-square-foot room—it had one window.

Since the twins were living on the facility and looking for things to do as their father worked, tennis became the obvious diversion. The talent displayed by both, but especially Frances, turned the diversion into an immersion. He began to receive coaching, and then extra coaching. Among the children of parents paying for their chance of becoming pros, he became the unexpected prodigy. In 2013, fifteen years after Federer won the prestigious Orange Bowl junior tennis tournament, Tiafoe at fifteen years old became the youngest boys' singles champion in its history. At seventeen, he played in the French Open and the U.S. Open on wild cards. These are amazing achievements for a young player but also achievements similar to those of many professional players you have ended up never hearing of. For every Federer or Edberg, who were absolutely dominant junior players, there are twenty dominant junior players who didn't make it at the highest level of the circuit and spend their careers battling it out on a rung below, the Challenger Tour. That said, Tiafoe has physical gifts that translate well to competing against the very best players in the world. His foot speed is peerless, his racket speed and the easy power it generates are impressive, his serve at such a young age is already a weapon.

He's aided by the fact that he seems to like to compete. A strong dose of Challenger tournaments far from the glitz of the ATP Tour has helped him. A young Nadal skipped out on junior tournaments in favor of hardening his game and himself on the Challenger circuit. Federer, Djokovic, and Murray were distinguished juniors. Wawrinka passed through juniors without making much of a dent. Every player is an island. When Tiafoe readied to return

Federer's serve at 3–5, 40–all in the fifth set, he was ranked seventieth in the world despite coming into the match with only three wins for the year on the main circuit; he had fattened up on points from Challenger tournaments in Dallas, San Francisco, Sarasota, and Aix-en-Provence.

As with any minor league, the Challenger circuit presents obstacles players on the ATP World Tour don't have to face. In his first-round match in Sarasota against fellow American Mitchell Krueger, serving up 6–3, 3–2 in the match, the distinct and unmistakable sounds of two people fucking suddenly began to pierce the air. They played on. The sounds went on for a couple of minutes. Mitchell eventually responded by picking up a tennis ball and smacking it out of the grounds in the general direction of the noise. It continued. Tiafoe, trying to get on with it and serve again, paused and then yelled out to himself, the crowd, and the source of sounds: "It can't be that good!" Then he spun the ball on his racket playfully, got on with it, and won the final three games of the match on the trot.

Of course, a Challenger match at the Sarasota Open isn't a match at the U.S. Open, and Tiafoe isn't immune to pressure. It was only a year ago that he was up two sets to none on John Isner, the perennial top-ranked American on the circuit in these days when an Agassi or a Sampras seems a distant memory. That was the debut for the new Grandstand, a medium-sized bowl-like stadium with views of the city skyline. The crowd pushed unabashedly for the charismatic kid as he swung from his heels and chased down everything, much to the increasingly obvious chagrin of the six-foot-ten Isner, a saturnine player who makes his living off his serve. Tiafoe served for that match at 5–3 in the third, but couldn't seal the deal. Then, after going to a tiebreaker in that same set, he led 1–3 and served at 5–5—the moments slipped away from the eighteen-year-old. As did the set. He was still up two sets to one but the loss washed over Tiafoe like a tidal wave. He lost the next two sets and the match. You could feel it coming after he lost the tiebreak in the third. Almost as if to emphasize the opportunity lost in the third set, Isner closed him out clinically in a second tiebreak, this one in the fifth set.

A year later, and he finds himself in a first-round U.S. Open match deep into the fifth set against the prohibitive favorite. He's a year older now and coming off the biggest win of his career to date, having taken down the seventh-ranked player in the world and hottest player on the tour, Sascha Zverev, in Cincinnati.

He is dressed in matte black from head to ankles, a thick black headband where his flattop starts its rise, his sneakers streaks of rouged pink. Still at the beginning of whatever path he's on in his life, he finds himself at the same big place but this time on a much bigger stage, Ashe, against much bigger competition, Federer, two sets all, 3–5 in the fifth, 40–all: two points from losing the match but also two points from edging toward a life-changing win. He watches Federer start his toss, bend his knees, twist into trophy position, and rise to meet the ball.

The deuce side of the court, the right side, offers three options for a right-handed server against a right-handed returner: serve wide to the forehand; serve directly at the body; or, the high-risk-high-reward option, go for the T right down the middle of the court. The risk is that it's the smallest of the three targets and missing it leaves you facing a more compromised second serve. The reward is that it's the most difficult shot to return, especially effectively, and it goes to the returner's backhand. If you hit your target on a T-serve, you're going to get an ace at best or, typically, a compromised backhand return—usually a player's weaker side. A serve directly to the body, which inexplicably appears to be used less these days, can surprise a returner who is expecting to have to move quickly, instinctively, to the right or left. There's no ace to be found in it, but a hard serve directly into the body is an excellent way to get a player to freeze, and it plants another seed of doubt in the returner's mind about where subsequent serves might go. The serve out wide to the forehand moves the returner off the court, opening up wide swaths of space for the server to play the ball into if and when the returner gets the ball back in play. It's a classic option for a player looking to finish off a one-two punch: move your opponent off the court with a wide serve, and then, when the ball comes back to you, take advantage of the returner being off the court. Nadal has long thrived on the left-handed version of this play. The risk involved with it is that if you miss your target, you've given your opponent numerous options off the forehand: down the line, aggressively cross court, deep and right back at your feet—it's a recipe for disaster.

Federer decides to go down the T.

The serve has spin for safe placement, which allows Tiafoe to jab-step twice to his left and hit an uncomfortable-looking two-handed backhand that bounces just behind the service line on the ad side of the court, deep enough to keep Federer pinned to the baseline. Federer loads up his one-handed backhand and sends a topspin reply deep and straight to the middle of Tiafoe's side of the court.

This is the start of a conversation under tense circumstances. No need to be rash. Instead, a prudent shot to see where things in this point are and where they might be heading. *Hey, Frances. How's it going? What do you want to do?* a shot like this implies, where the questioner plans time to feel out the response.

Tiafoe sees Federer's reply coming right down the middle of the court and takes two steps backward, prepares his forehand. The choice is Tiafoe's now. Left? Right? Straight back down the middle?

High risk? Or with a safe margin? Aggressive and flat? Or defensive, with tons of spin? Tiafoe chooses to hit the ball right back at the crouched Federer, who had remained where he was, shading ever so slightly toward the ad court on his left. Having seen that his return is in, Tiafoe steadies himself and crouches into ready position. He is standing three feet behind the baseline now. He'll stay there.

Federer takes Tiafoe's neutral reply with his forehand, this time letting loose a heavy, topspin shot that lands deep in the corner, making Tiafoe move and find the ball with his backhand; by the time he reaches it he's three feet behind the doubles alley. But Tiafoe's foot speed makes getting to this ball easy. His feet process information quickly and turn Federer's shot out wide more into a nuisance than a real inconvenience. Tiafoe has to move, but he gets there in plenty of time and sends back to Federer a strong backhand response.

The conversation changes now.

His feet know something Federer can't possibly know at this moment: they see the pattern that Federer sees, they're reading his mind.

Normally, Federer shouldn't and probably doesn't care.

Tiafoe's backhand does what it does best at this stage of his career: it holds the fort. Tiafoe twists into a two-handed shot from the doubles lane that he sends safely back, right back, where Federer was standing. Federer's third shot from the same spot of the court is the change of rhythm—a punctuation mark before the final statement. He uncorks a sharp forehand straight across the court from where he's standing. It's not down the line, as Federer wasn't down the line; but it's close to it and it's hit with venomous pace. Tiafoe has no time to sprint the length of the court to get to Federer's forehand.

Tiafoe sprints the length of the court and gets to Federer's forehand.

Federer's no fool. Stubborn, but no fool. He knows Tiafoe is fast. And the forehand he hit, dangerous but safely inside the line, is designed to turn out the lights on Tiafoe before saying good night. Tiafoe may well get to the shot. If he doesn't, the point is over: advantage Federer. If he does, sprinting all that distance won't get him in position to hit anything back that would trouble Federer. And that's when he'll look to say good night. Maybe Tiafoe will get to it and loop something tamely back that Federer will meet at the net and pluck out of the air. Or maybe he'll feel pressed and go for a shot he can't possibly hit—a winner right back down the same line, for instance—and spray the ball wide. Same difference. Same result.

Tiafoe is running with his racket already drawn back to hit a forehand. It's the proper technique. You do this so that you don't waste time and motion when you arrive to the ball, your racket at that point already drawn back so you just swing at it. It's the proper technique, but to see Tiafoe do it emphasizes what a mess his technique is. Imagine a surfer standing on a board, arms bent and out, turning his trunk to change direction in the water. This is what the Tiafoe forehand looks like. His racket preparation allows him to hit the ball with both tremendous pace and spin as it stresses in his motion the action of brushing up against the back of the ball. It's effective and unsightly. You see all of the coaches in his ear, touching his forearm, holding his elbow as they guide him through one practice swing after another, changing from one swing to another, textbook to arcane and back again. But there are things you can't coach. This is one of them.

His racket is behind him, the stringbed parallel to the court. This is, for now, the point of his life. He's sprinting with ridiculous speed, it's almost laughable how fast he's moving. A black kid in black being a black blur on Arthur Ashe's court. He cups the ball waist-high with his racket, catching it more on its side than on its back, and sends the ball back across the net at a forty-five-degree angle.

It finds the singles sideline of the right service box. As it kisses the white tape, it seems to veer off farther away from the court and pick up speed.

Federer starts to sprint after it as though he can reach it, as though he hasn't seen what he's just seen, but his mind catches up to what's happened and you can see him slightly drop his head while his body still dutifully moves to the right. Then the ball skids off to nowhere. No, not nowhere. Toward a corner exit. It was done with the match and with all of us. It bids us all adieu.

Now 5–4 in the fifth. Advantage, once again, Tiafoe.

Federer had faced this scoreline just two points earlier. When he wiped it away with an ace down the T we ended up where this story started: deuce. But Tiafoe's capitulation didn't come with it. Just like when he broke Federer in the first game of the match, as the crowd still filed in and the stadium reeked of noise, he held on and won the set. And just like when he lost the second set 1–6 and the third set 2–6, which was the expected capitulation, he pushed back and won the fourth set in kind, 6–1, when the last thing Federer wanted to do was play five sets in the first round of the U.S. Open in the middle of the night and coming off tweaking his back. Federer wanted this to end as soon as possible. And it wouldn't end. Not because he was sloppy but because Tiafoe answered the bell. Federer has offered Tiafoe four break chances up to this moment. And Tiafoe has taken three of them.

So it's 5–4 in the fifth. Advantage, once again, Tiafoe. Federer once again goes down the T. Tiafoe stretches to reach it and send back another deep, safe return almost to the same exact spot

as the last point but this time with his forehand. Federer is impatient here. Enough of this. He whips the same forehand he had
hit before straight across the net.

Tiafoe's on fire. He's on autopilot. Federer knows the same
shot he just hit for a winner is coming. But now that he knows
it's coming it'll be easy to deal with. He charges in. He'll snuff it
out at the net.

The answer instead comes down the line. With clarity and
pace. Federer never saw it coming. Federer has offered Tiafoe five
break chances up to this moment. And Tiafoe has taken four of
them. Game, Tiafoe. The crowd, which had been half enthralled,
half expecting the usual outcome, had come to life again with
Tiafoe's scooped crosscourt winner the point before. Now they
are beside themselves. The chatter between points has stopped. A
roar erupts with the break. Jonathan roars along with everyone
else; amid all the cheering I only hear one word he says: *heroic*.
Tiafoe, soaked in adrenaline, continues his baseline sprint all the
way to his chair. They had played nine games in the set and it was
time to switch sides. Tiafoe could serve now for 5–all in the fifth.
Five–all in the fifth. After that he'd see another service game
from Federer, who was unrecognizably shaky with his serve.
Anything could happen.

Then, the most likely thing happens. Federer finds his way
straight into the biggest service game of Tiafoe's young career:
30–40—match point for Federer.

Tiafoe blasts a body serve at him, which Federer blocks back
with his backhand, just short of the same spot of the court where
all of the action had been for Federer in the prior game. But the
return is a little short and Tiafoe's feet push him forward to find
it. Before he knows it he's between the baseline and the service
line: the rough waters of no-man's-land.

There is no right shot in this position at this score against this player in this place at this hour. Any shot is on the table, as long as it keeps the story going. Something with safety to it, but not soft. Something that allows you to reset and get home, weigh your options, grow into the point. And here, finally, Tiafoe's feet fail him. He shapes up to spin a forehand to his right. Then twists at the last moment to hit one straight up the line or slightly to his left. His feet, processing the information, go out from under him. The ball goes meekly into the net. Federer looks neither joyous nor relieved, more concerned. Tiafoe has played a menacing match, he knows; but something is not right. Tiafoe looks down at the court, shrugs at it with the wave of the arm of the betrayed. But then he quickly gets over it. Heads to the net. Where he and Federer hug and walk off out of sight.

U.S. OPEN EPILOGUE

Dušan Lajović. Taro Daniel. Leonardo Mayer. Andrey Rublev. Alexandr Dolgopolov. Juan Martín del Potro. Kevin Anderson.

These are the players Rafa Nadal beat to win the 2017 U.S. Open.

The highest-ranked among them was del Potro, who staged the type of comeback that you wouldn't believe even if you saw it against Dominic Thiem while felled almost to his knees by the flu. Down 1–6, 2–6 and facing match point down 3–5 in the third, he then emptied his tank in a stunning display of resilience and power to beat Roger Federer in a four-set quarterfinal. Out of gas and lacking the right weapons against a rested Nadal, he gave everything to win the first set 6–4, then faded, his competitiveness spent, the match soon taking the feel of pitch-and-catch.

The average ranking of Nadal's seven opponents was sixty-three.

RANKING	MOVE	PLAYER	AGE	POINTS	TOURN PLAYED	POINTS DROPPING
1	–	Rafael Nadal	31	9,465	16	0
2	–	Roger Federer	36	7,505	16	0
3	–	Andy Murray	30	6,790	18	0
4	–	Alexander Zverev	20	4,310	23	0
5	–	Marin Čilić	28	4,155	22	0
6	–	Novak Djokovic	30	4,125	17	0
7	–	Dominic Thiem	24	3,925	27	0
8	^1	Grigor Dimitrov	26	3,575	24	0
9	v1	Stan Wawrinka	32	3,540	17	0
10	–	Pablo Carreño Busta	26	2,855	25	0
11	–	Milos Raonic	26	2,825	21	0
12	–	David Goffin	26	2,650	26	0
13	–	Roberto Bautista Agut	29	2,525	25	0
14	–	Kei Nishikori	27	2,475	21	0
15	–	Kevin Anderson	31	2,470	22	45
16	–	Sam Querrey	29	2,445	22	0
17	–	John Isner	32	2,425	24	0
18	–	Jo-Wilfried Tsonga	32	2,375	21	0
19	–	Tomáš Berdych	32	2,355	23	250
20	/	Nick Kyrgios	22	2,245	20	0

Official ATP rankings, September 25, 2017. (www.atpworldtour.com)

He lost a total of three sets.

It was his sixteenth Grand Slam and his third U.S. Open title. He entered the tournament as the top-ranked player in the world, exited the tournament as the top-ranked player in the world, and would end 2017 as the top player in the world.

For some reason, the tournament never caught fire. Anderson was the last man standing on the other side of the draw. It was loud outside and loud inside. It came and went. There wasn't much more to it. As we say in New York, whether we love tennis or not: It is what it is.

Nadal vs. Dimitrov at the Rolex Shanghai Masters quarterfinals, October 13, 2017. (Photograph by Lintao Zhang / Getty Images)

THE ASIAN SWING

Real autumn comes just before the clocks change, before all the drastic adjustments to the encroaching darkness. That's autumn frozen in time. Picturesque autumn of any century but this one, which feels like it's left autumn behind but for that thin line of time when the Asian swing happens and the mornings indulge themselves with long, blue 7:45 a.m. sunrises, and the days feel more like summer going slowly through the motions of becoming winter than a season unto itself. If you live in New York, as I do, it can feel like tennis has gone away and won't be back for a long while.

Tennis ceases to come up casually here after the U.S. Open. The final Grand Slam plays out like the final scene in a film, the fourth piece in a four-part puzzle.

But the circuit rolls on. After the final scene there are the credits and something more—special things. And yet, it's true that tennis becomes more intimate at this point of the year. Especially in 2017, when the Australian Open became a type of tennis therapy played out in public. In a few weeks, when the cold really comes, I'll be back to playing on a red clay surface called Fast Dry in an indoor bubble under the Ed Koch Bridge. And I'll be starved for a good match on the television and the casual conversations with people who'd seen some big Grand Slam match. January will come again, then, and reset everything.

But these weeks between late September and early October are when the tour becomes a time for the players like no other point in the year. After nine months' worth of results, the Asian swing is when a player can step away and see the shape his season has taken—whether he'll wait to dip 2017 in amber or drop it in the trash. Chengdu-Shenzhen, Beijing-Tokyo, and then Shanghai: these form the bridge where the circuit crosses over fully into realms of personal glory. Everyone dreams of the Grand Slams, and for that reason they are for everyone; they are as much the fan's dream as the player's. If you tune out after New York, you miss the season-defining questions that come after. There's still time to rise or fall in the rankings with all the personal heavens or hells that come with it. There's still time to finish at a career-high number, in the top one hundred, top fifty, top twenty, top ten. There's still time for a very select few lucky souls to qualify for the über-prestigious ATP Finals in London that conclude the year. Still time, unbelievably it should seem, for Federer or Nadal to end the season at number one.

This is also the newest part of the circuit. The Japan Open, founded in 1972, is the elder statesman. Chengdu was founded just in 2016. Shenzhen in 2013. And Shanghai in 2009. This newness has allowed the swing to tuck itself sensibly into this part of the calendar, following a neat big-bigger-biggest format: the two 250 tournaments—Chengdu and Shenzhen—are played simultaneously; followed by, again simultaneously, the 500s in Beijing and Tokyo; and then the Masters 1000 in Shanghai closes out the swing.

And it's here, as the circuit began to near its end, that 2017 started to circle back to its beginning.

Chengdu ended up being won by the player who first set the alarm bells of the 2017 season ringing by beating Djokovic in the second round of the Australian Open. All the way back in January, Denis Istomin had made the draw in Melbourne as a wild card. The week prior he was playing in a Challenger in Bangkok, where he lost in the second round. Thirty years old, ranked 117th in the world, and coached by his mother, Klaudiya Istomina, he had been born in Russia but plays under the flag of Uzbekistan. Istomin stood tall against Djokovic, hung with him stroke for stroke, and played the big points as if he and not his opponent were a six-time champion of the tournament. And this wasn't the knackered Djokovic we'd come to see later in the year: he'd played one tournament beforehand, Doha, and won it. Djokovic acknowledged Istomin's superiority after the match: "All the credit to Denis for playing amazing," Djokovic said. "He deserved to win. No doubt, he was the better player in the clutch moments. He stepped it up, played aggressive. Served very well, very precise. There's not much I could do." For his part, Istomin was more circumspect about the best win of his career to date. Asked how he did it, Istomin responded, "I don't know, actually, how I did it."

He may not have known, but he followed it up by beating thirtieth-ranked Pablo Carreño Busta of Spain in the following round. Carreño Busta would go on to have a career year in 2017: at the start of Chengdu he was ranked tenth in the world.

The victory against Djokovic in particular was the type that, for players ranking in the hundreds, would be the highlight of their season. But when I asked my friends if they'd rather win an early-round match at a Grand Slam against the favorite or win a 250, they unanimously chose the 250. (For the record, I'd choose the slam upset.) Istomin didn't end up having to choose: he started the year with one and closed the year with the other. Admittedly, he didn't do much at the other majors, but so be it. As much as the start of the year turned all of the focus back on Federer and Nadal, this year was also for the Istomins on the circuit. He started 2017 as the 121st-ranked player in the world and ended it ranked 63rd. As long as he remains hovering at that number going forward he'll be an automatic entrant into the Grand Slams, Indian Wells, and Miami.

He played the Cyprian Marcos Baghdatis in the final. Baghdatis was the number-one-ranked junior player in the world in 2003 and a former rising star on the tour. He climbed as high as eighth in the rankings in 2006, but he is now perhaps best known for his guest-starring role in the final win of Andre Agassi's career in that year's U.S. Open. Agassi's autobiography *Open* uses his 6–4, 6–4, 3–6, 5–7, 7–5 win as a framing device for the story of his life in tennis, and Baghdatis plays the role of emergent talent personified in irrepressible, lovable youth, which is funny inasmuch as Baghdatis sported the same well-insulated frame back then that he does now. In the end (spoiler!) the intensely physical demands of the match and their unwillingness to yield got the best of both of them. They finished the five sets on their feet but barely made it back to the adjacent medical tables in the trainer's room to receive IVs for their cramps. They held hands there, tennis having brought the old master and young artist together in joy and pain.

Eleven years later, Baghdatis was the old soul in the Chengdu final. He was in his third final in the past three years, having made it that far at Dubai in 2016 and Atlanta in 2015—but he hadn't won a title since Sydney in 2010. The year 2017 was firing off warning signs to Baghdatis about the state of his career: he arrived at Chengdu having lost in the first round in seven of the fifteen tournaments he'd played on the circuit, and, to add insult to ignominy, on day one of the tournament the latest rankings revealed that he'd dropped out of the top one hundred for the first time since October 2014. But he'd been better of late, having played tough in St. Petersburg, Winston-Salem, and Washington, D.C. And he had to like his chances against Istomin, who, aside from an uptick in Gstaad, seemed to have blown his wad of good luck in Melbourne.

Six games into the Chengdu final, serving at 2–3, 15–all, Baghdatis sprayed a forehand down the line wide and the Cypriot's face took on a look not of disappointment or frustration but of bitter recognition. He bent at the waist a few times and then continued. On the next point, he took a few exaggerated deep breaths and hit a serve as hard as he at that moment could, and when the return headed back toward him he halfheartedly swatted at it as you would a gnat. He collapsed to his knees, slowly, taking up a prose of supplication—knees to chest, facedown, arms out in front—that changed to dismay: he began to pound the court with his fists. His back had given out. I watched Baghdatis prone on the court, bent over in no-man's-land, and I couldn't help but think of his moments in *Open* when even though he lost, his body could give everything it had for him; and I couldn't help but think back to Istomin's skill set giving everything it had for him to defeat Djokovic in January. Agassi became Djokovic's coach in 2017. I wonder what the two of them would have thought had they been watching this abbreviated match together as it was happening.

Either way, Denis Istomin was the 2017 champion of Chengdu. After, he'd make the semifinals of a Challenger in his native Uzbekistan, but he wouldn't win another ATP Tour match for the rest of the year. Baghdatis would make it back to action two weeks later and win a round-of-thirty-two match at the Stockholm Open, and that would be the end of things for his year on the circuit as well. But Chengdu ensured them both direct entry into the 2018 Australian Open. And once there, they would both make the second round, earning a cool $70,560 each.

Meanwhile, 1,056 miles due southeast toward the coast of the South China Sea, past Guangzhou and Dongguan, lies Shenzhen, a mere ten and a half miles from Hong Kong. Although a 250-class enterprise just like Chengdu, Shenzhen has lacked for top-of-the-draw star power over the four years of its existence. Andy Murray won the first iteration of the tournament in 2014 and Tomáš Berdych won in 2015 and 2016. Neither could play in 2017. The top seed coming in was Sascha Zverev, who, still getting accustomed to such things perhaps, fell in the quarterfinals to Bosnia and Herzegovina's top player, Damir Džumhur. The older Zverev, the left-handed serve-and-volleyer Mischa, was the third seed and lost in the second round to Israel's Dudi Sela, a pocket rocket of a player with a surprisingly effective one-handed backhand for someone of his size. Sela is also another well-traveled player in his early thirties who becomes especially dangerous during the back end of the circuit. Goffin was the second seed and made his way through the draw untroubled until the semifinal, when he needed three sets to get by the Finnish-Swiss Henri Laaksonen. This set up a final with someone from the first pages of this book: none other than Alexandr Dolgopolov.

Things in 2017 had gone extremely well for Dolgopolov since that early date with Nadal in Brisbane. He won a 250 on the clay of Buenos Aires, beating Carreño Busta and Nishikori to take the title; he made the quarters of Rio, where Carreño Busta would exact some revenge. He made the final of the Swedish Open in Båstad, beat eventual U.S. Open finalist Kevin Anderson of South Africa in the big tune-up in Cincinnati, and made it to the round of sixteen in New York, where he'd lose once again to Nadal.

After an early exit in the 250 tournament between Cincinnati and the U.S. Open, the Winston-Salem Open, Dolgopolov came under scrutiny from the Tennis Integrity Unit (TIU) due to an alarming swing in online betting activity during his match against Thiago Monteiro of Brazil. In short, Dolgopolov was playing an opponent who had never won an ATP Tour–level match on hard courts and he lost 3–6, 3–6, spraying errors on his groundstrokes and managing not one single break-point opportunity in the match. (The only two other times this had occurred in his career were against Federer, one of the most dominant servers in the history of the game.) Two hours before the match was set to start, online bets on it drifted so dramatically that gambling sites began removing betting on the match, meaning they sensed something wrong. Some websites continued to offer bets on the match and the odds continued to drift up to minutes prior to the match, inviting play on a Dolgopolov loss: the money had moved Monteiro from the big underdog to the big favorite. In the fourth game, he was broken after double-faulting on back-to-back points. By now more betting sites were removing the match from play and connoisseurs of tennis gambling across the globe—they are legion—were live-streaming the match to catch a glimpse of what all the noise was about concerning what should have been an innocuous first-round match at a 250 tournament. Afterward, Dolgopolov would provide testimony to the TIU and face a very curious press corps at the U.S. Open. He denied all wrongdoing, chalking up the bad result to fatigue and pacing himself for the U.S. Open. When asked in New York what he thought about all of the circumstantial evidence surrounding the suspicions of match-fixing, he replied, "You want my honest answer? I don't give a fuck to be honest because it's like a circus."

On the court, the essential elements of funk and improvisation still powered his game, but it was blending nicely with smart decision making, which allowed Dolgopolov to show off his tennis IQ and his above-average athleticism. Things were clicking for him.

Amazingly, he still didn't have a sponsor for his racket. In fact, not only did his stringbeds not have a stencil on them, it looked to the naked eye like he was playing with a batch of older rackets. They showed signs of wear and tear across the top as well as up and down the sides, and a chunk of the bumper was gone. He still used what looked like Wilson Pro Staffs and still walked out onto the court with a Wilson bag similar to Goffin's, whose fate had changed completely from when he was last seen on clay: injured and Horacio Zeballos carrying his bag back into the locker room for him.

The final was a fight marked by little degrees that swung the match in Goffin's favor. Dolgopolov tried to discomfit Goffin with topspin forehands designed to push him back, then opening the court for the Ukranian's assortment of drop shots and slice. But Goffin now had found that little measure that would rocket him into the top ten. He was catching those high bouncing balls early, before they reached the peak of their ascent, and redirecting them flatter and with pace. Fully healed from his ankle injury, he was even leaving his feet at times to get on top of a ball he wanted to send back with authority. He was hitting out more and seeking the initiative in points during moments where before he was more liable to politely continue the exchange with a safer groundstroke. Now more than ever, Goffin was hitting aggressively into safe targets. And, being the technician that he is, safe targets for him are closer to the line than most. The formula got him past a red-hot Dolgopolov and was key to his lifting the trophy in Tokyo, too. The only bad thing about winning consecutive tournaments is that there's a third tournament right after to play. With so much tennis in his legs, doing much of anything in Shanghai was too tall an order and he lost to France's Gilles Simon in the round of thirty-two. However, everyone was going to have their hands full in Shanghai. Nadal had entered the ring at Beijing and beat Pouille, Khachanov, Isner, Dimitrov, and Kyrgios to win the title, add another 500 points to his lead on Federer, and get a head start on the final stretch of the year. Federer would show up for Shanghai and Shanghai alone. Its courts are some of the fastest hard courts in the world, fast like they used to be and not the plodding composite used in places like Miami. He was fond of it, it flattered his game. And he seemed to genuinely love the city. He would lose one set there.

A magnolia in autumn, the Rolex Shanghai Masters is the penultimate of the nine Masters 1000 tournaments played throughout the year and the only one in Asia. It's played in a large bowl called the Qi Zhong Stadium, whose interior is ringed by blue and red seats, a purple hard court centered on a bright green bed, and, up above it all, a beautiful retractable roof made of eight curved wedges that as the roof starts to close slowly twist to meet in the middle and clasp together overhead like a spiral galaxy. For the first five years of the stadium's existence the tournament was named the ATP Tour Masters 1000 Tournament of the Year. This is the tournament I wake up to on those autumn mornings when there's less dawn light and more of a chill in the air. In a way it marks its own special end to the circuit, in that it's the last outdoor tournament of the year.

Shanghai began on the eighth of October. Ten months ago

to the day, I woke up with the big things in tennis as they had been for a while. Djokovic and Murray had just battled it out in a final in Qatar. Who would have guessed then that we'd be where we were now? Maybe there were signs in the little things in tennis. Like how ten months ago to the day a small 250 in Sydney started what would end with thirty-three-year-old Gilles Müller of Luxembourg winning his first-ever title after nearly sixteen years on the tour. He'd go on to win a second title, this time at 's-Hertogenbosch, and then perhaps top both by beating Nadal at Wimbledon in the round of sixteen by gutting out a 15–13 victory in the fifth and final set. (Remember, at Wimbledon they don't play tiebreakers in the final set.) "I'm just glad it's over," Müller said after the match. "Somehow I made it."

And somehow the circuit had made it to Shanghai. It had been a strange brew of the monumental and the minimal that had gotten us here. Some of the yardsticks had been buried in the ground— the biggest ones: we know who won the majors. But that didn't matter to Shanghai, did it? Why would it? Shanghai wants its say, too. It had been a long year, in tennis and outside it. And now, before tennis headed back to the indoor arenas of Europe, Shanghai was at once a hello and a goodbye to all that. There were still things in play and to play for, things to motivate players on the final turn in a long run that had turned into a sprint.

Zverev had already qualified, continuing his run of youngest-since-Djokovic feats over the course of the year. Four players arrived in Shanghai with a chance to be the eighth and final player to qualify for the final tournament of the year, the 1,500-point ATP Final in London. In eighth place at the moment was Goffin, which was even more impressive considering he'd missed six weeks of the season. But he'd returned and was closing out the year in peak form. Thus far for the year, he'd played eight matches in Asia and won eight matches in Asia, having won the titles in Shenzhen and Tokyo back-to-back. Hot on his tail were Querrey and the U.S. Open finalist Kevin Anderson.

And then there were Federer and Nadal. Federer was set to play his first tournament since losing to del Potro in New York. Nadal played Beijing between New York and Shanghai, beating a flustered Kyrgios 6–1, 6–2 in the final and bagging 500 additional ranking points for the effort. That made 149 weeks at number one in the world over the course of his career. He was playing out the year with an eye to extending that further. McEnroe had 170 weeks. Djokovic 223. Connors 268. Lendl 270. Sampras 286. And Federer, up until that point in October 2017, had spent 302 total weeks at the top of the rankings. Neither Nadal nor Federer were defending points, as both had been injured at the end of 2016. For 2017, Nadal had a healthy lead on Federer and didn't have to worry about points dropping off. Any points picked up from here on were gravy.

The Shanghai quarterfinals were among the best of the year. Nadal and Dimitrov staged a sequel to their semifinal at the Australian Open, with Nadal once again having that little bit extra to win. The volatile Troicki put his considerable skills on display in Shanghai by dispatching the young Canadian phenom Shapovalov by bageling him in the third set, edging Thiem and Isner in a third-set tiebreaker, before pushing del Potro to the distance, then succumbing to him, the Argentine in the end being too much and in too rich a vein of form for him. Čilić also won a routine victory against another surprise quarterfinalist in Ramos Viñolas.

And then there was Federer-Gasquet. This was one of my favorite matches of the year due to the fact that you rarely encounter two top players as distinctive and yet similar as these two. They both have beautiful one-handed backhands, but Federer's is more a weapon and Gasquet's more an instrument. The new Federer approach of hitting through the backhand to produce a flat groundstroke that cuts through the court differs greatly from Gasquet's single-hander, which is loaded with spin. One backhand is like a name printed in bold and the other is in cursive. Their forehands are similar, but Gasquet's is set for stun, while Federer's is set for kill. You would think, then, from this description that Federer would simply bludgeon Gasquet, but it's not simply how you choose to hit the ball that matters, it's also where you choose to stand. Federer, as we've gone over, hugs the baseline now at all costs and even half-volleys short-hops if he needs to; all of this is designed to rob his opponents of time and also keep his impetus going toward the net so that he can sneak in at the right moment and finish off a point with his polished net game. On the other hand, Gasquet tends to position himself two to three feet behind the baseline, sometimes more. This gives him not only extra time to respond and react to his opponent's shots, but also the space and distance for the looping backswing his topspin groundstrokes require to carve through the court on both vertical and horizontal planes. Gasquet has been a fixture on the tour since 2002 after a decorated career in the junior ranks. He's won fourteen titles and made the semifinals of Wimbledon and the U.S. Open, the quarterfinals of the French, and four times has been to the fourth round of the Australian Open, and he has qualified for the ATP Tour Finals twice. And yet, when you consider Gasquet's strengths, it's easy to see his weaknesses as well. He stands too far back in the court, and the beauty of his groundstrokes comes at the expense of pace. This makes him tough opposition for players below the top twenty but compromises his chances against higher-ranked players. The beauty of the 2017 quarterfinal in Shanghai was more aesthetic. Federer's 7–5, 6–4 win over Gasquet pushed him to 16–2 in their all-time matchups. But it was fascinating to put Federer's backhand in context when he plays another player with a single-hander, and Gasquet truly prides himself on the optics of the shot. Federer's groundstrokes take the ball early, causing the spin his shots generate to be less pronounced to the observer. Gasquet, meanwhile, from his drawback to his follow-through seems in terms of playing style a cousin of Federer's. With his modern racket and strings he produces spin and arc we wouldn't otherwise be able to see, but the grace and ballet approach hark back to an earlier idea of tennis as a type of ballet with a moving target. His approach is beautiful and works more often than it doesn't. But then, as much as a score like 7–5, 6–4 tells a story of a match decided by small differences, when Federer broke Gasquet late in the first to practically close out the set and then broke him in the second, got broken back, and then broke him again, I remembered that the only two times Gasquet had ever beaten Federer had been via third-set tiebreakers on clay. I had been drawn once again into the flickering flame that is watching Roger Federer. I thought I had escaped, but I hadn't.

Federer would go on to meet del Potro in the Shanghai semi-final, lose the first set 6–3, and beat him in the next two 6–3, 6–3. Although Nadal and Djokovic have beaten Federer far more often than del Potro has, no one has done more damage to Federer than del Potro, with those two U.S. Open upsets in 2009 and 2017. Neither defeat had enhanced or further humanized Federer, as many of the losses to Nadal and Djokovic had done. No, del Potro simply beat him. He has been the Trojan horse in the men's game for going on a decade. He's a gift to the circuit. But you never know what's inside him on any given day, often until it's too late. Federer learned this the hard way twice, and his career has been forever changed for it. He's beaten del Potro far more times than he's lost to him: he's won eighteen times—and lost only six—including the four-and-a-half-hour marathon on Centre Court in

RANKING	MOVE	PLAYER	AGE	POINTS	TOURN PLAYED	POINTS DROPPING
1	_	Rafael Nadal	31	10,465	16	0
2	_	Roger Federer	36	8,505	16	0
3	_	Andy Murray	30	5,290	17	0
4	_	Marin Čilić	29	4,505	22	0
5	_	Alexander Zverev	20	4,400	24	0
6	_	Dominic Thiem	24	3,935	27	0
7	_	Novak Djokovic	30	3,765	17	0
8	^1	Grigor Dimitrov	26	3,590	23	90
9	v1	Stan Wawrinka	32	3,450	16	0
10	_	David Goffin	26	2,885	26	90
11	_	Pablo Carreño Busta	26	2,855	24	250
12	_	Milos Raonic	26	2,600	21	0
13	_	John Isner	32	2,550	25	0
14	_	Sam Querrey	30	2,525	22	0
15	_	Kei Nishikori	27	2,475	20	0
16	_	Kevin Anderson	31	2,470	21	45
17	_	Jo-Wilfried Tsonga	32	2,285	19	0
18	_	Tomáš Berdych	32	2,230	21	0
19	_	Juan Martin del Potro	29	2,225	18	250
20	_	Nick Kyrgios	22	2,010	19	0

Official ATP rankings, October 16, 2017. (www.atpworldtour.com)

Wimbledon: a 3–6, 7–6 (7–5), 19–17 match at the 2012 Olympics that's been described as the greatest Olympic tennis match ever played. But del Potro's six victories are like gut punches and resonate. In 2009, Federer was riding a streak of five consecutive U.S. Open titles. When he played del Potro in the final, he won the first set with ease: six games to three. But then the big Argentine won tiebreakers in the second and fourth sets and then took the fifth set in a stroll. After years recovering from his numerous wrist surgeries, he played the 2016 Rio Olympics hardly match-fit and took out Djokovic in the first round, sending the Serb off the court in tears. In this year's U.S. Open he was up to more of the same, first against Thiem and then again against Federer. Rarely has someone so large and so obviously in possession of rare gifts of raw power slipped so easily into the underdog role and enjoyed widespread support from fanatics as well as neutrals. Something about his game and demeanor draw people in. Part of it is that he often looks like he can't continue playing even when he's fine; it's just his body language, he's a languid guy. Part of it is that he has a true flair for the dramatic and appears to play his best on the biggest stages. And part of it is simply that he's ridiculously good. He's still only twenty-nine as I am writing this, and yet so much of his twenties were taken from him—and from us—due to injury. What could have been. And yet, what still can be.

Here in Shanghai he was continuing his resurgence, after numerous surgeries on both wrists. Federer may have slowed del Potro's momentum, but it was good to see him back. He's a problem for any top player, not merely a bad matchup for one or two. Any draw is richer with him lurking in it. Hopefully, by the time you're reading this, *resurgent* isn't a word accompanying del Potro. Hopefully, he's simply there. If there is such a thing as simply being there.

TWILIGHT INDOORS

There are stories. And then there are stories. The twin reemergence of Roger Federer and Rafa Nadal in 2017 has been one of those story-stories, full of wait-that's-not-alls and tell-me-what-happened-nexts. Their return to form together has been as emphatic, as unexpected, as a jolt of sun at the start of a strange year.

When the two faced off in the final of the Australian Open back in January—which Federer won in a tense five sets 6–4, 3–6, 6–1, 3–6, 6–3—there was the sense that the stars had simply happened to align for one last, fleeting time. Federer was ranked and seeded seventeenth at the time; Nadal hadn't reached the semifinal of a major since 2014. It was supposed to be lightning caught in a bottle, something to be savored before reality set back in.

But since then Federer and Nadal have played three more times, including in two other finals. They even played on the same team—as doubles partners, no less—in a team-tennis enterprise in Prague dreamed up by Federer called the Laver Cup, after the Australian great Rod Laver. Most recently, they played in the final of the Rolex Shanghai Masters. Nadal was in imperious form coming into that final, having just won the previous tournament in Beijing and the one prior to that, some minor summer event played in Queens. When they flipped the coin at center court in Shanghai, Nadal hadn't lost in seventeen matches. Federer won in straight sets in barely over an hour: 6–4, 6–3.

The last time they'd played before that was in the final in Miami in late March: Federer won in straight sets in barely over an hour: 6–3, 6–4. Prior to that they had played only a couple of weeks earlier, with Federer winning in straight sets . . . in barely over an hour: 6–2, 6–3.

In other words, the last three times they've played, Federer has dry-erased Nadal. And in the only close match they played, in Melbourne, Federer sped past Nadal in the final five games. The severity and consistency of these beatdowns have been aided greatly by the fact that Federer had skipped out on the clay court season entirely and watched from afar as Nadal won his tenth title in Monte Carlo, his tenth in Barcelona, his fifth in Madrid, and, in Paris, his tenth French Open. So, where exactly are we with

these two? Quiet as it's kept, we're at the point where we can't tell if it's better that these two keep playing each other, or whether they should be kept as far apart from each other as possible. Nadal is ranked number one in the world. Federer is number two. Nadal at this point can't touch Federer. Federer may never again play on clay. And, aside from a moment of divine intervention on the other side of the net, the other players on the tour can't keep up. Another story in the story of 2017. And all this with winter coming.

Now, after ten straight months of chasing the sun and living in a floating bubble of perpetual summer, the ATP World Tour—the official name for the highest category in tennis of the men's professional circuit—has turned the final corner and veered, at last, into autumn. Call me strange and unredeemable, but this is one of my favorite times of the tennis season. The grand narratives of the majors—who will win or not win what? how will that affect this person's or that person's legacy?—have come and gone. We know by now all about the miraculous returns of Roger Federer and Rafa Nadal. Not only did they split the four majors up for grabs this year, they're certain to end the season ranked in the top two. Most of the remaining hierarchy—Djokovic, Murray, Wawrinka, Nishikori, Raonic—have been out injured. The others—Čilić, Zverev,

Grigor Dimitrov, Nitto ATP Tour Finals, London, November 19, 2017. (Photograph by Naomi Baker / Getty Images)

Thiem, del Potro—have alternately flickered and faded on the biggest stages. Nothing has come close to vying with Federer and Nadal for the spotlight, and nothing that happens between now and the end of November could possibly change that.

Therefore, aside from some vague love of tennis for its own sake, what really matters now, with the U.S. Open fairly far in the year's rearview mirror? And what about it is beautiful, now that 2017's story has been all but written, the matches from now until the end of the year being played out in the dreary pall of one indoor arena after another?

Exactly.

This is the time of the tennis season that has fewer of the fun baubles of tennis in it—no cheery sun, no wind, no anachronistic traditions, and match after match on one unremarkable, and for the most part interchangeable, indoor backdrop after another. No more late-winter dreamscapes of the Coachella Valley, no more Mediterranean vistas behind the mezzanine in Monte Carlo, no more impossibly red strawberries on beds of frothing cream in the thimble-sized London summer. This is the tour distilled to its most unromantic elements under the advancing autumn nights and the encroaching darkness of Moscow, Antwerp, Stockholm, Basel, Vienna, and—like lovers who didn't know better than to leave well enough alone—less-sexy second swings through Paris and London in November to close out the year.

And in the end, the end was like the beginning: the same player who won the first tournament of 2017 won the final tournament of 2017. Bulgaria's Grigor Dimitrov, aka Baby Fed, defeated David Goffin in the London final, a futuristic affair played under electric-blue atmospheric lighting. How fitting that a player who modeled his game on Federer would bookend the year, and not Federer himself. Or Rafa. At its heart, the 2017 year in tennis is about inspiration, not supplication; renovation, not repetition.

RANKING	MOVE	PLAYER	AGE	POINTS	TOURN PLAYED	POINTS DROPPING
1	_	Rafael Nadal	31	10,645	18	0
2	_	Roger Federer	36	9,605	17	0
3	^3	Grigor Dimitrov	26	5,150	23	0
4	v1	Alexander Zverev	20	4,610	25	0
5	v1	Dominic Thiem	24	4,015	27	0
6	v1	Marin Čilić	29	3,805	22	0
7	^1	David Goffin	26	3,775	26	0
8	^1	Jack Sock	25	3,165	22	0
9	v2	Stan Wawrinka	32	2,615	15	0
10	_	Pablo Carreño Busta	26	2,595	25	0
11	_	Juan Martin del Potro	29	2,585	19	0
12	_	Novak Djokovic	30	2,535	16	0
13	_	Sam Querrey	30	2,480	23	0
14	_	Kevin Anderson	31	2,320	22	0
15	_	Jo-Wilfried Tsonga	32	2,290	20	0
16	_	Andy Murray	30	2,265	16	0
17	_	John Isner	32	2,235	24	0
18	_	Lucas Pouille	23	2,095	24	0
19	_	Tomáš Berdych	32	2,015	19	0
20	_	Roberto Bautista Agut	29	2,010	24	0

Official ATP rankings, November 20, 2017. (www.atpworldtour.com)

Time will tell if the year of Roger and Rafa was really under the surface the year of Grigor and David; or Sascha, Nick, and Frances. That's a question the next cycle of seasons will answer. In tennis and in life.

Now is the time when life starts to press closely. And tennis seems more momentary, more fleeting, the pastoral sucked from it. It's a sober denouement back to a Europe of clenched fists, toxic fear of its own shadow, and the bleating cacophony of useless, cowardly politicians. Tennis comes back to this like a returning prodigal. It, too, has had its role to play in what 2017 was and will be remembered as. Just remember: this is not the dawn of heroes, it's the dusk.

That is, if we let it be.

So don't let it be.